PRAYING
CONSTANTLY

PRAYING CONSTANTLY:

BRINGING YOUR FAITH TO LIFE

FATHER BENEDICT J. GROESCHEL, C.F.R.

Our Sunday Visitor Publishing Division
Our Sunday Visitor, Inc.
Huntington, Indiana 46750

REJOICE ALWAYS, PRAY CONSTANTLY,
GIVE THANKS IN ALL CIRCUMSTANCES,
FOR THIS IS THE WILL OF GOD
IN CHRIST JESUS FOR YOU.

— 1 Thessalonians 5:16-18

Dedication

In grateful remembrance of the many authors
who have enriched my life through their writings on prayer.

Acknowledgments

I would like to thank Father Patrick Fitzsimons and Father
Paul Chavasse, C.O., who read early drafts of this book. Their
comments and criticisms were of great assistance to me. I am also
especially grateful to Bert Ghezzi of Our Sunday Visitor, who first
suggested that I write a book such as this. His advice, patience,
and insight proved instrumental in completing *Praying Constantly:
Bringing Your Faith to Life*, and I appreciate his efforts greatly.

— Father Benedict J. Groeschel, C.F.R.
July 15, 2010
Feast of St. Bonaventure

Contents

Introduction

I have no doubt that many of those who will read this book will be people who have already realized that prayer is an essential part of their lives. Perhaps some have converted from sinful lives or, at least, from lives that seemed lackluster — somehow devoid of something essential. Perhaps some were always nominally Christians but lived their faith in a distracted or perfunctory way. Others may have led very respectable and even rather devout lives but have arrived at a second conversion, so to speak. They may have reached a point where they can see their relationship to God, to Christ, and to the world around them in a different and clearer light. Usually, these people are older and are searching for something deeper than the transitory joys that seemed so important to them when they were young. Some may even have good reason to be looking forward to the end of their earthly lives, and they want to be prepared. This turning to God and to prayer in one's later years is so common that we are often surprised and impressed when we meet a young person in his teens or early twenties who is truly fervent and committed in a religious sense. In our time, this is considered a special grace.

This book, as well as all the books I've ever written, is addressed specifically to this group of people, no matter what their age: the more committed, more fervent part of the population, those who — unlike so many in our time — are aware of the presence of God in the world and specifically in their lives. I know this group includes many Catholics, but it is certainly not limited to Catholics; it includes Christians from all denominations and even, at times, non-Christians as well. I have written for this audience for more years now than I care to count, and I hope people have found some help and perhaps a little inspiration from my books. If this is so, it is only due to the work of the Holy Spirit. By the way, please don't blame the Holy Spirit for any mistakes you may find in my work. Any inspiration you derive from my books comes from the Spirit. I'm able to manage the mistakes entirely on my own.

In this book, we will examine some advice given by St. Paul. It is necessary advice, but this advice is also very challenging and not a little awesome. His command in his first epistle to the Thessalonians is to "pray without ceasing" (v. 5:17, NAB). What in the world can that mean, and how can any human being hope to accomplish such a feat? Often, this statement of St. Paul is rendered in a simpler but even more demanding way: "Pray constantly." As such, it seems impossible. It is discouraging to read these words in Holy Scripture, for in them God seems to demand something from us of which we are not capable. I hope that in the course of this book we will come to see that such discouragement is not really necessary.

When I was young, I must confess, I got myself into some trouble by trying to take these words of St. Paul not just seriously but too literally. At the present time, I see some of the things I did in my early efforts to "pray constantly" as having much less to do with genuine prayer than they did with obsessive-compulsive behavior — but excess is one of the great temptations of youth. I did not stay very long in this attempt because I quickly realized that it had become a distraction from my responsibilities and the normal life of a Christian person. My instincts finally led me to study psychology, and this taught me that there are forms of religious experience that can be unsound and maybe even a little crazy. I was forced to conclude that attempting to "pray without ceasing," in a very literal way, was among them. As I said, I didn't try it for very long.

Despite this early obsession regarding prayer, time and time again these powerful words would come back to me: "Pray constantly." Whenever I contemplated them, I still wanted them to be true for me; I wished I could examine my daily experience and find in it constant prayer in some way or some form.

Over the years I have come to learn many things about prayer; I have also come to experience prayer in ways that are different from those of my youth. I am sure many people reading this book have had similar experiences. Yet, can I truly say that I know what it is to "pray without ceasing?" Can we even truly say that prayer without cease is possible for beings affected by original sin? In this little book we will attempt to find the answers to those questions and to others that we will encounter along the way. We will try to find ways to fulfill the daunting words of St. Paul (or at least to approach fulfilling them). In doing so we follow the prayerful example of many great Christians who have preceded us and who have yearned for lives of endless prayer. As we begin our journey, we remind ourselves that we walk in the footsteps of saints and mystics.

CHAPTER ONE

GOD ON THE INITIATIVE

Cast me not away from thy presence,
    and take not thy holy Spirit from me.
Restore to me the joy of thy salvation,
    and uphold me with a willing spirit.
O Lord, open Thou my lips
    and my mouth shall show forth Thy praise.

— Psalm 51:11-12, 15

THE PARADOX OF PRAYER

Ultimately, prayer — like everything that is good — is a gift from God. It is a grace. Although we may desperately want to pray, we must remember that we cannot do so without God's help, for we do not ever initiate real prayer. We never pray alone. True prayer always finds its source in God and is really a response to God's reaching out to us, to His grace extended to us. St. Paul speaks very clearly of this in his epistle to the Romans:

> Likewise the Spirit helps us in our weakness; for we do not know how to pray as we ought, but the Spirit himself intercedes for us with sighs too deep for words. And he who searches the hearts of men knows what is

> the mind of the Spirit, because the Spirit intercedes for
> the saints according to the will of God.
>
> — Romans 8:26-27

Here, St. Paul shows us that although prayer is our turning
to God, it depends totally on God's prior calling to us.

Throughout the ages, many have seen and understood
this seeming paradox of prayer. Abraham Joshua Heschel,
the twentieth-century Jewish religious thinker who attended
the Second Vatican Council as an observer, once wrote:

> There is something which is far greater than my desire
> to pray, namely, God's desire that I pray. There is
> something which is far greater than my will to believe,
> namely, God's will that I believe. How insignificant is
> the outpouring of my soul in the midst of this great
> universe! Unless it is the will of God that I pray, unless
> God desires our prayer, how ludicrous is all my praying.[1]

The Church has understood and pondered this for
centuries. In the *Catechism of the Catholic Church*, we find
this idea stated in a very beautiful way using imagery from
St. John's account of Jesus' encounter with the Samaritan
woman at Jacob's well.

> The wonder of prayer is revealed beside the well where
> we come seeking water: there, Christ comes to meet
> every human being. It is he who first seeks us and asks
> us for a drink. Jesus thirsts; his asking arises from the
> depths of God's desire for us. Whether we realize it or
> not, prayer is the encounter of God's thirst with ours.
> God thirsts that we may thirst for him.[2]

These are startling words if we really stop to think about them. Here, the Church tells us that our prayer, which we often dismiss as insignificant or even empty, is not empty at all. Before we have even uttered a word, our prayer is already full of "God's thirst" for us, of His love for us, of His desire to be in constant, intimate relationship with us. The moment we truly realize this about prayer, we are well on our way to "praying constantly."

THE NOISE OF THE WORLD AND THE STILLNESS OF PRAYER

Despite all this, we must be realists. Prayer is difficult. In our contemporary world we are too often unaware not only of God's thirst for us but even of our own thirst for Him. Prayer is often forgotten: God's call to us to turn to Him in prayer goes ignored or unheard. We live frantic lives that keep us rushing from one task to another. Our days are cluttered with constant and often unimportant activity. Cell phones and the Internet intrude, even when we are alone in our cars. Text messages bombard us with meaningless chatter from which we can find no escape. The whisperings of God become drowned out by the incessant noise of the world. What can we do in such a situation? How can we pray if we barely have time to think?

> How can we pray if we barely have time to think?

"Be still and know that I am God" (Psalm 46:10), the psalmist tells us, reminding us that prayer demands an end to chatter, an end to distraction, a focus on what really matters. Prayer requires of us that we hear — if only for an instant — the "still small voice" (1 Kings 19:12) of God calling to us, for this voice offers us a way to live that is different from the one the world offers — different and infinitely better.

For most of us, the first stage in learning to pray well must be to face the fact that, in our world, prayer really has become difficult. In some ways it may be more difficult than ever before. Prayer has become something more often spoken about than done because we have become deaf to the voice that calls us to prayer. Christ still waits for us at the well, but He often waits there alone and in vain. Often, we become aware of the impulse to pray only when we are faced with great need — when disaster has struck and the limitations of our own powers (and all earthly power) are clearly and painfully revealed to us.

I am writing these words only days after an immense earthquake has devastated Haiti, already the poorest and most desperate country in the Western Hemisphere. The news reports are moving, startling, and profoundly disturbing. Destruction is everywhere. Yet I have seen photographs in the newspapers of this disaster that seem filled with hope: people kneeling in the street, surrounded by rubble, their arms outstretched in prayer, imploring the help of God. Even the secular newspapers spoke of the fervor and faith of many ordinary people in the face of this disaster in Port-au-Prince. These people were suffering enormously and seemingly very unfairly, yet they were not cursing God, and they were not giving up. Instead, they were turning to God and finding hope in despair and the courage to go on. Where then did such prayer begin? In their desperate prayers, these people were responding to graces being abundantly bestowed on them in the midst of their tragedy.

But how does one respond as these poor people did? Must we wait for the day when disaster turns our world upside down in order to pray well? How can we learn to turn from the meaningless noise of the world and respond to God in the stillness of prayer? These are the questions we will try to answer in this book.

HOW CAN WE PRAY?

What allows us to pray? What permits us to turn to the call of God? First of all, in order for us to pray, we must have some belief in God, or at least an impulse toward that belief. We must have some sense of the reality of God. To the atheist, the ultimate basis of all reality is nothingness, meaninglessness, randomness. Such an attitude obviously rules out prayer, making it nonsensical — because in such an understanding, prayer is an attempt to communicate with no one, a turning towards nothing, a response to emptiness. Agnostics are different, but not really all that much better. They lack belief in God, yet some desire to believe remains — a faint remnant of hope in the Divine.

From time to time, agnostics are driven to prayer by the difficulties of life; but for them, prayer is an embarrassment, a sad soliloquy, a yearning for something they would like to believe but cannot. I certainly have known agnostics who have tried to pray. It's a strange and rather sad thing to listen to. It usually goes something like this: "God, if you're there, please listen to me." This is not a particularly inspiring beginning — but it is a beginning! We should never overlook that, and we should never forget that God has built huge edifices on much smaller foundations than this.

> "One cannot pray unless he has faith in his own ability to accost the infinite, merciful, eternal God."

If we do not believe or at least hope that God is real and that God can and does listen to us, attempts at prayer will be not only empty but frustrating.

There are people in the world known as deists, who believe in God or at least accept the possibility of God. However, they also believe that God is so far removed from the world that He has no effect on our lives, that He does not hear prayer and is neither aware of our needs nor concerned with our existence. To the deist, God created the universe with all its physical laws and then departed from it, leaving it to run on its own.

This is a very philosophical approach to religion, and obviously is not very satisfying. In fact, it is cold and frightening. As is true for the agnostic, the deist cannot really pray, for although he believes God exists, the deist believes that God does not care about us, that man and God are permanently alienated from each other, separated by an unbridgeable gulf. Heschel wrote:

> The issue of prayer is not prayer; the issue of prayer is God.
> One cannot pray unless he has faith in his own ability to
> accost the infinite, merciful, eternal God.[3]

This is absolutely true — and the deist, like the agnostic, believes that he cannot "accost" God, that God is indifferent to his needs and deaf to his call.

Most people, however, do not find themselves in the predicament of the agnostic or the deist. Most people believe in or at least sense the reality of God, and they do not believe that man is so estranged from God that no contact is ever possible between the human and the Divine. In other words, the vast majority of people in the world are theists of one sort or another. This means that they not only believe in the reality of God; they also believe that God is aware of us and cares about us, that God can and does hear us and respond to our needs. All true Christians are theists by definition; so are all real Jews and Muslims.

But Christian theism is different from other kinds of theism. It understands God in a deeper way than other forms of theism can. To the basic concepts of theism, Christianity adds the profound belief in the Most Holy Trinity. The Christian knows that God exists not in solitary isolation, but in dynamic relationship — in love. As Christians, we believe that when we speak to God, we speak to the three persons within God: the Heavenly Father; the Divine Word who is Jesus Christ, the incarnate Son of God; and the Holy Spirit. This God, who is in constant relationship, is the only God to whom the Christian calls out in prayer, the only God in whom the Christian places all his trust. When a Christian prays, therefore, he understands his prayer to be a way of entering into relationship or of deepening a relationship with God.

> When we speak to God, we speak to the three persons within God: the Heavenly Father; the Divine Word who is Jesus Christ, the incarnate Son of God; and the Holy Spirit.

LIVING IN THE PRESENCE OF GOD

Along with crying out to God and praying to God is the belief that one can actually live in the presence of God. In the very first pages of the book of Genesis in the Old Testament, we read that man was created in the image of God. One of the ways in which we can understand this amazing statement is that relationship is as fundamental to our being as it is to the being of God. Without relationship with others, and especially relationship with God, we cannot live truly human lives. Every real relationship involves expectations, things required of those in the relationship. This is certainly true when it comes to our relationship with God.

Jesus promised that if we keep up our part of the relationship by obeying his commandments, he will enable us to live in God's presence. He tells us this very clearly in the Gospel of St. John when he says:

> "He who has my commandments and keeps them, he it is who loves me; and he who loves me will be loved by my Father, and I will love him and manifest myself to him.... If a man loves me, he will keep my word, and my Father will love him, and we will come to him and make our home with him."
>
> — John 14:21, 23

PRAYER OF REPENTANCE — COMING BACK INTO GOD'S PRESENCE

A person may nevertheless severely damage his relationship to God by falling into serious sin. But such a person will always be aware that he has turned away from God — that his human weakness or, perhaps, his malice has ruptured this all-important relationship.

It has been my experience during more than a half century of priesthood that most of the time, believers who fall into serious sin do so with a certain reluctance and an almost immediate dissatisfaction with themselves. Therefore, they are apt to arrive at a position of repentance rather quickly. Being in a state of serious sin is a painful and disturbing experience for them; they are aware that they have lost something important and profound, and they feel a great need to repair the damage they have caused. This condition usually arises through sins of weakness, and people cry out to God to forgive them and restore their relationship with Him. As they cry out, they are once again praying, again responding to God, who is constantly calling on them to turn back to Him and to His law. The prayer that asks for forgiveness is probably among the most common prayers that we utter, and this must be the case for all who are afflicted by original sin.

Such people who sin, but then turn back to God, are blessed — even if they have sinned seriously, because God is always ready to forgive those who sincerely repent. There are also, however, frightened people who are aware of God or at least suspect that there is a God, but deny this and live their lives as if He does not exist. They turn their own desires into their god and live only according to them. They ignore the real God, of whom they are at least dimly aware, and they ignore His commandments.

There is a teaching of the Church that states that God gives all people the basic ability to discern the fundamental principles of the moral life. This is called the natural law. The Fathers of the Church expressed this by saying that the commandments are "engraved on the hearts of human beings." Therefore, except for a very small and unfortunate group known as psychopaths, people can be said to be aware of the difference between right and wrong.

Even mentally ill people are able to recognize this distinction most of the time. The psychopath, perhaps, is *able to do it from time to time in an intellectual way, yet he does not internalize this knowledge and so feels no impulse to obey God's commandments. The psychopath is one who thinks he is without responsibility. Without any doubt, a psychopath is an extremely dangerous person. The great and terrible wars that took place during the twentieth century were obviously rooted in the actions of psychopaths.*

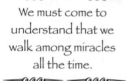

We must come to understand that we walk among miracles all the time.

To pray constantly, or even regularly, we must cultivate an awareness of God's presence within us and around us. And as we become more alive to the Divine Presence, prayer will become more and more natural to us.

In the beginning, we must remind ourselves that God's holy presence suffuses all things and every aspect of our lives. We must consciously look for traces of God in the world around us, in our relationships with others, in the events of our lives. We must learn to see the world around us with new eyes, realizing that in the changing of the seasons, the movements of the stars and planets, and the growth and development of all kinds of life, we are witnessing God's continuing creation unfold before us. We must come to understand that we walk among miracles all the time. All things come from God, so all things should remind us of God, and we should praise God constantly for the great mystery of creation.

CHAPTER TWO

PRAYING IN GOD'S "ABSENCE"

As a hart longs for flowing streams.
>   so longs my soul for thee, O God.
My soul thirsts for God,
>   for the living God.
When shall I come and behold the face of God?
My tears have been my food day and night,
>   while men say to me continually,
"Where is your God?"

— Psalm 42:1-3

In centuries past — during the Middle Ages, for example — I suspect that praise (and prayer in general) was more possible and more readily attainable than it is for many people today. Those times were often called the Age of Faith, a name that describes them well. The population of Europe then was not just Christian but profoundly Catholic. The sad divisions within Christianity had not yet come into being, so almost everyone shared a basic religious understanding. Few would have claimed that God did not exist; few would have said that Jesus was not His Son. Everything was seen through very Christian eyes, and all things were understood to be kept in existence by the loving will of God. I suspect that the Divine Presence was almost palpable for many people then.

Today, we live in a world of a thousand competing visions of reality. Some of these visions, as we have already noted, are sterile: they leave no room for God. In our own time, best-selling books have titles like *God Is Not Great* and *The God Delusion*. Such books tell us — indeed, they shout at us — to abandon all faith in God. Many people, including important scientists, have an exclusively materialist understanding of the universe, one that completely rejects the spiritual dimension of existence — the dimension of real depth. The reality of God seems to be an open question (or a question that has been definitively answered in the negative) for far too many people in our troubled time — including, unfortunately, some clergy.

A few decades ago, "Death of God" theology became inexplicably popular in many Protestant seminaries. At roughly the same time, a Jewish rabbi became famous for teaching that God is best understood as "Holy nothingness"[4] — certainly not an easy concept to pray to. A famous Protestant bishop, who has made a career and (no doubt) large sums of money by regularly attacking the faith he has sworn to uphold, has very publicly written:

> Theism, as a way of defining God, is dead. So most theological God-talk is today meaningless.

The same man tells us:

> Prayer cannot be a request made to a theistic deity to act in human history in a particular way.[5]

These statements are sad — and, if we think about them for a while, we realize they're also somewhat silly. They really amount to shallow theological fads that come and go, but even after they go they leave behind them a residue of doubt, a question mark constantly hovering over all that is important in life, making everything seem uncertain.

Perhaps there is a small part of many of us hiding deep inside that does not or cannot completely believe in the God to whom we want so desperately to pray.

All this cannot help but create ambivalence in the minds of many people who desire to pray, even many devoutly religious people. Perhaps there is a small part of many of us hiding deep inside that does not or cannot completely believe in the God to whom we want so desperately to pray. This is very understandable, considering the world in which we live. But if our souls are divided in this way, if our faith is very flawed and weak, prayer will become difficult and tentative. It may even appear foolish to us, or we might be tempted to think of it as a waste of time. Perhaps it may even become little different from the prayer of the agnostic we spoke of above.

This uncertainty may not be understood as the lack of faith that it really is in the minds of many. Instead it may make us feel that God is not present, or that God has somehow withdrawn from us like the God of the deist. We may feel that we pray (as Shakespeare wrote) to a "deaf heaven." We try to pray, but we can't help but think that our prayers are not heard or at least not received in love. We become angry at God, who seems so silent, and we feel alone and helpless. Finally, we echo the thoughts of the American poet Emily Dickinson, when she wrote:

> Of Course — I prayed —
> And did God Care?
> He cared as much as on the Air a Bird — had stamped
>   her foot —
> And cried "Give Me" —[6]

I suspect that everyone who is reading this book has experienced at least one moment when the words of this poem seemed to express the truth about prayer. Every human life is confronted by difficulties, even tragedies, that threaten to overwhelm us. We have all prayed desperately — perhaps at the bedside of a dying loved one —begging God to intervene and prevent our world from shattering. And often we have felt that the God to whom we pray has turned far from us just at the moment we needed Him the most, that the absence of God has become more real than His presence.

The very profound and spiritual Orthodox writer Archbishop Anthony Bloom has written of this problem:

> Obviously I am not speaking of a real absence — God is never really absent — but of the sense of absence which we have. We stand before God and we shout into an empty sky, out of which there is no reply. We turn in all directions and He is not to be found. What ought we to think of this situation?[7]

No matter how much we may feel lost or alone, or even inhabiting a world from which God seems to have withdrawn, we must never forget Archbishop Bloom's statement that "God is never really absent." The very existence of the universe around us proclaims not only the presence but also the love of God.

We must also not forget that, no matter how intense our pain, we are not the first to feel abandoned, as we can see from the following anguished words taken from the biblical book of Lamentations: "Though I call and cry for help, he shuts out my prayer" (Lamentations 3:8). We have only to look to the psalms to find many instances of this sense of being lost, of being forsaken by God. The following quotations are but a few of the many that express this:

> We have only to look to the psalms to find many instances of a sense of being lost, of being forsaken by God.

O God, do not keep silence;
   do not hold thy peace or be still, O God!

— Psalm 83:1

Why dost thou hide thy face?
   Why dost thou forget our affliction and oppression?

— Psalm 44:24

[W]hy has thou cast me off?
Why go I mourning because of the oppression of
   the enemy?

— Psalm 43:2

My tears have been my food day and night,
   while men say to me continually,
      "Where is your God?"

— Psalm 42:3

Of course, the best-known example of this is the Twenty-second Psalm, the first line of which is identical to Jesus' cry of dereliction on the cross:

> My God, my God, why hast thou forsaken me?
> Why are thou so far from helping me,
>> from the words of my groaning?
> O my God, I cry by day, but thou dost not answer;
>> and by night, but find no rest.

— Psalm 22:1-2

In these difficult and heartrending words, we find impassioned prayer to a God who seems impossibly distant and unwilling to respond. But we also see that this is the anguished cry of someone who never doubts the existence of God and who perseveres in prayer, trusting that his prayer will ultimately be heard — that God can, in fact, answer him. For the psalmists, God may often have seemed distant or even absent, yet they had the courage to believe that it was always possible to encounter God if one did not lose hope but persevered.

The first line of Psalm 63 shows this clearly:

> O God, thou art my God, I seek thee,
>> my soul thirsts for thee;
> my flesh faints for thee,
>> as in a dry and weary land where no water is.

— Psalm 63:1

Here, we see that it is God's presence that bestows life, that a relationship to God is as essential to the human soul as water is for the human body. In this psalm, the author continues to search for God, never doubting that at the right moment God will disclose Himself.

Psalm 130 begins with the famous line, "Out of the depths I cry to thee, O LORD!" (Psalm 130:1). The psalmist is in the depths of despair, yet he finds hope even in despair and has the courage to say, "I wait for the LORD, my soul waits, and in his word I hope" (Psalm 130:5-6). We find here a faith so strong that it conquers the hopelessness that inevitably results from a life without God. Even in the "depths," the psalmist waits in confidence for God, who only seems to be absent.

We, too, must maintain hope in both the reality of God and in God's overwhelming love for us. We must remember that the terrifying feeling that God is absent is not unique to us but is common. We must accept the fact that it is a mysterious part of God's plan for us.

At times of dryness, or when we feel abandoned by God, we must do all we can to persevere. This attitude of perseverance in prayer, in fact, is essential at all times, at every moment of our lives — even during those wonderful moments when God feels close to us. Pope John Paul II points out a perfect model for this perseverance. It is that of the apostles, gathered in company with the Blessed Virgin and the other disciples in the upper room after Christ's Ascension into heaven. His Holiness writes:

> The prayer of the community of the apostles and disciples before Pentecost was persevering: "They devoted themselves to prayer." It was not a prayer of momentary exaltation. The Greek word used by the

author of the Acts of the Apostles suggests a patient assiduousness, in a certain sense even a "stubbornness," implying sacrifice and the overcoming of difficulty. It was therefore a prayer of the most complete dedication, not only of the heart but also of the will.[8]

Like the psalmists before them, the apostles persevere in their prayer. They call upon God in confidence, over and over, knowing that they will be heard and answered in ways beyond their imagining. In the Holy Father's words regarding this, we find what our attitude toward prayer must be, whether we feel abandoned by God or blessed by His presence. At all times we must pray, knowing that in prayer we find the one relationship that can truly give us life. We must be as "stubborn" and "assiduous" as the apostles and await the God who "is never really absent."

CHAPTER THREE

WHAT DO WE MEAN BY "GOD"?

> Whither shall I go from thy Spirit?
>   Or whither shall I flee from thy presence?
> If I ascend to the heaven, thou art there!
> If I make my bed in Sheol, thou art there!
> If I take the wings of the morning
>   and dwell in the uttermost parts of the sea,
> even there thy hand shall lead me,
>   and thy right hand shall hold me.

— Psalm 139:7-10

THE MYSTERY OF GOD

As we undertake to obey St. Paul's exhortation to pray constantly, we must come to a clearer understanding of the God to whom we pray. Who is God? What is He like? How do I dare approach Him? Let's reflect on these questions in this chapter.

Almost every human being — from oriental monks, Buddhists, and Hindus, all the way to militant atheists — has a word or words for God, for the Divine Presence. Even those who deny Him have some kind of an idea about God (or at least about gods). "God" is the most important word in the human vocabulary. Once in Germany in the early

1930s, the Jewish religious thinker Martin Buber was told that he should eliminate the use of the word "God" in order to make his writing more accessible to those who did not believe. Incensed, Buber immediately responded: *"Aber Gott ist ein Urwort!"*[9] ("God is a primordial word!") In other words, he was saying that "God" is a word that we cannot do without.

> "God" is the most important word in the human vocabulary.

The Christian believer must have a clear idea of what he means when he says the word "God." This idea must be very different from that of the polytheist, for whom there are many gods, each with great power but none with ultimate power. It must be radically different, as well, from the ideas often found in eastern religions in which God is vague and ambiguous. In such religions, God is often understood not to be personal but almost an abstraction, an undifferentiated being, a divine abyss, or totally immanent in the universe. This is the god of pantheism, of whom the Christian writer C. S. Lewis wrote:

> The pantheist's god does nothing, demands nothing. He is there if you wish for him, like a book on a shelf. He will not pursue you.[10]

Some recent Protestant theologians have advanced ideas which seem to be along pantheistic lines, calling God "the ground of being," "the power of being," or, simply, "being."[11] While these ideas have a certain type of theological validity, they seem to reduce the personhood of God, to make God somehow inferior to man. If we think of God in these terms, we will inevitably imagine a Creator who has somehow become less than His creatures — a ridiculous paradox! We will also arrive back at the pantheist's god who exists but who does nothing, who will never pursue you or wait for you at the well — who can never truly love you or call you by name.

It is certainly impossible to pray to a God whom we consider sub-personal. To be a true Christian is to believe in the Holy Trinity, and thus in the concept of personhood in God. But we must also be careful to remember that personhood in God is not like the personhood of a human being.[12] Human personhood is the only kind of personhood with which we have any direct experience (and we don't even fully understand that). So we must remember that when we apply the word "personhood" to God, we do so only as an analogy or a symbol. Personhood in God infinitely transcends that of man.

From our perspective, God is infinitely supra-personal. In fact, even when we use a term like "supra-personal" in referring to God, we must always be conscious of the fact that we are falling far short of the truth, for superlatives inevitably become diminutives when applied to the divine reality.

> God is the infinite, mysterious presence who completely fills the universe, yet extends immeasurably beyond it.

If our ideas about God become too ambiguous — if we find ourselves thinking of God as being excessively immanent or non-personal — genuine prayer will become very difficult, if not almost impossible for us. To the Christian and the Jewish believer, God is the infinite, mysterious presence who completely fills the universe, yet extends immeasurably beyond it. This idea of God is famously expressed by St.

Paul, who cites the ideas of the pagan philosopher Aratus: "In him we live and move and have our being" (Acts 17:28). Here, we see that the Divine Presence pervades all but is different from all.

Unfortunately, we often ignore this astonishing fact. One finds rather accomplished and even apparently gifted people who can go for weeks and even months without even stopping once to reflect on the fact that they are living in the Divine Presence, that their very existence continues from instant to instant only because of the Divine Love, that God is closer to them than their own heartbeat. Perhaps one feels more compassion for the person who believes, yet does not think of God, than for the one who doesn't believe at all.

The people who would be inclined to read a book such as this one, of course, are of the sort that strives to know God and to live actively in His presence. These are the people who have begun to be hungry for prayer, for a deeper relationship with God: They are the ones who want to meet Jesus at the well. They are not satisfied to pray from time to time or even to begin and end each day with prayer. Instead, they find themselves engaged in prayer of one kind or another over and over again throughout the day. Perhaps they say specific prayers; perhaps words of prayer leap spontaneously to their lips; perhaps prayer comes wordlessly, as a yearning or just an awareness of the Divine Presence; perhaps prayer occasionally grasps them unexpectedly for reasons they don't understand. It doesn't really matter, as long as they respond to the call to prayer that is with us at all times.

THE HUMAN FACE OF GOD

Our fellow monotheists, Jews and Muslims, pray to the great King of the Universe, the infinite Sovereign. To them, God is formless, unimaginable, beyond all comprehension, concealed by and possessed of a majesty too immense and extreme to be comprehended by human beings.

We see this concept of a distant God expressed perfectly in the book of Exodus during the theophany at Mount Sinai. God's presence is revealed by thunder and lightning and by deafening, blaring trumpets — but God Himself remains unseen; only the manifestations of His power are able to be perceived by man. "You cannot see my face, for a man shall not see my face and live," says this mysterious and distant God (Exodus 33:20). For this reason, among others, Jews and Muslims use no images at all, and in their prayers they sometimes seem to us to relate to God as if to a faraway monarch, one who can be only partially encountered.

One of the most famous Jewish prayers is the *Kaddish*. Said in various forms repeatedly during every daily Jewish prayer service, it shows this characteristic clearly. Following is a short quotation from one of the frequently used versions of it:

> Hallowed and enhanced may He be throughout the world of His own creation. May He cause His sovereignty soon to be accepted, during our life and the life of all Israel. And let us say: Amen.
>
> May He be praised throughout all time.
>
> Glorified and celebrated, lauded and worshiped, acclaimed and honored, extolled and exalted, may

the Holy One be, praised beyond all song and psalm, beyond all tributes which mortals can utter. And let us say: Amen.[13]

As Catholics, we find this style of prayer too formal, too distant. To us, it seems to be prayer to a great King (which we know God to be) but not to a loving Father (which we also know God to be). The great difference between Christian prayer and the prayer of other monotheists is Christ, Himself. In his letter to the Galatians, St. Paul expresses this perfectly:

> But when the time had fully come, God sent forth his Son, born of woman, born under the law, to redeem those who were under the law, so that we might receive adoption as sons. And because you are sons, God has sent the Spirit of his Son into our hearts, crying, "Abba! Father!" So through God you are no longer a slave but a son, and if a son then an heir.
>
> — Galatians 4:4-7

Here, we find that the relationship between God and man has been radically altered through the life, death, and Resurrection of Jesus. It is through Him, St. Paul tells us, that we have received "adoption as sons" of the Father. We no longer need to address the Father as if we were mere subjects of the Divine King. With Jesus, we can now address this King intimately as *"Abba."*

In Christ, we meet God not as ineffable spirit or limitless creative power, but as a man, a tangible reality to whom we can pray.

It is always through Christ, the Word made flesh, that we approach the Father; in Christ, we find the human face of God, a face we can see and love. In Christ, we meet God not as ineffable spirit or limitless creative power, but as a man, a tangible reality to whom we can pray, who can speak to us and call us over and over again back to the right road. We meet Christ in the words of the Gospel. We meet Him as a person who lived a human life and who gave Himself for us in a horrifying death. In the face of Christ, we find the true image of God, the God whose love for us is so great that, in the words of St. Paul, He "emptied himself, taking the form of a servant, being born in the likeness of men" (Philippians 2:7).

In Christ, we encounter not only the God who reigns in the high heavens in endless, unperturbed serenity, but the God who loves us, yearns for us, and even suffers for us. It is Christ who enables Christian prayer to be different from all other prayer and enables us to enter into a profoundly intimate relationship with God. As we contemplate Christ in Scripture, and especially in the Eucharist, prayer will become ever more personal for us, more natural to us, more real to us. It will become more and more like what Christian prayer must be: a loving relationship with another person.

THE PRESENCE OF THE HOLY TRINITY

The question we must face now is one of awareness, for the greater the awareness of God and the presence of God, the greater the possibility of prayer. How can we grow in that awareness of God? One way, as we have said, is to be very clear in our meaning when we speak of God, either to others or to ourselves in our private thoughts or in our prayers. I have already used the word "God" many times in this book and called it the most important word in our vocabulary.

Despite this, you will be surprised to know that I do not think that, for the Christian, it is generally a good idea to overuse that word. If we know God through Christ, we must incorporate this profound awareness into our prayer life.

For the Christian, the Blessed Trinity — impossible as this divine reality is to comprehend — can never be an abstraction. We cannot think of the triune God simply as a theological puzzle or a religious enigma. In order for our prayer to be real and deep, we must be aware of the presence of the Blessed Trinity in our lives and the lives of others. I believe that many devout believers are able to accomplish this, at least to a certain degree. For them the members of the Holy Trinity are often felt as present during their lives on earth.

> In order for our prayer to be real and deep, we must be aware of the presence of the Blessed Trinity in our lives and the lives of others.

If we know the three Divine Persons, equal to but distinct from each other, we must use this knowledge and focus our prayer on one of these Persons. We must never forget that each member of the Holy Trinity is, in fact, a distinct Person, although one perfectly united in substance with the other two. In God, there is one nature, the divine nature; there are, however, three Persons: Father, Son, and Holy Spirit. Since our prayer should be personal, we should pray to the individual Persons of the Holy Trinity.

When a Christian uses the word "God," whether he is consciously aware of it or not, he is usually addressing God the Father. When he wishes to speak to the Divine Word, the Son of God, the Second Person of the Holy Trinity, he will, of course, usually address Christ directly. When he wishes to invoke the Third Person of the Trinity, he will address the Holy Spirit as his Advocate and Comforter.

THE IMPORTANCE OF PRAYING TO THE INCARNATE WORD

While it is theoretically possible to pray to the Second Person of The Blessed Trinity without actually taking into account the fact that Christ entered human history as the incarnate Jesus of Nazareth, it would be most unusual to speak to the Logos, the Divine Word, in this way — in effect, ignoring the human face to God. In general, I would say not only that Christians have no need for such prayer, but that it can even become dangerous.

The great St. Teresa of Ávila, a doctor of the Church, warned against such prayer, and I agree with her completely. It brings us back full circle to the type of prayer that characterizes Judaism and Islam — prayer to a disembodied and awesome divinity — rather than the intimate conversation that is possible between a human person and Christ. The Incarnation has been given to us as the greatest fact of history and the means by which we are saved. Why, then, would we want to ignore it?

A Christian can, however, meditate profitably on the Logos, the Eternal Word. In fact, if we look at the readings the Church offers us for many feast days of Our Lord and Our Lady, we discover something very much like this. Often, these readings are drawn from the Wisdom literature of the Bible. The following is the reading from the Book of Proverbs that the Church offers us on the Solemnity of the Most Holy Trinity:

[Thus speaks the Wisdom of God:]
"The Lord created me at the beginning of his work,
    the first of his acts of old.
Ages ago I was set up,
    at the first, before the beginning of the earth.
When there were no depths I was brought forth,
    when there were no springs abounding
        with water;
Before the mountains had been shaped,
    Before the hills, I was brought forth;
Before he had made the earth with its fields,
    or the first of the dust of the world.
When he established the heavens, I was there,
    when he drew a circle on the face of the deep;
when he made firm the skies able,
    when he established the fountains of the deep,
when he assigned to the sea its limit,
  so that the waters might not transgress
      his command,
when he marked out the foundations of the earth,
    then I was beside him, like a master workman;
and I was daily his delight,
    rejoicing before him always,
rejoicing in his inhabited world
and delighting in the sons of men."

— Proverbs 8:22-31

The Church has always read this and many other such passages as referring to the Second Person of the Blessed Trinity. Wisdom here is the Eternal Word, through whom all things were made.

> Reading and pondering such Scriptural passages can be very helpful, but I must emphasize that they can never bring us as close to the Second Person of the Blessed Trinity as can prayer to the Incarnate Christ.

IMAGES OF GOD AID OUR PRAYER

Countless images of Christ's face have been made over the centuries. They are familiar to everyone. We can have no concrete image of God the Father in the way that we can of Christ. And the Holy Spirit, the Third Person of the Blessed Trinity, offers us few images that we can use as we reach out to Him.

However, many images of the Father have been attempted, both poetically and visually. One of the most compelling verbal images is found in the book of Daniel in the Old Testament. This is the image of the Father as "Ancient of Days":

As I looked, thrones were placed
    and one that was ancient of days
        took his seat;
his raiment was white as snow,
    and the hair of his head like pure wool;
his throne was fiery flames,
    its wheels were burning fire.
A stream of fire issued
    and came forth from before him;
a thousand thousands served him,
    and ten thousand times ten thousand stood before him;

the court sat in judgment,
and the books were opened.

— Daniel 7:9-14

In these biblical words, we find an image of God the Father that is already very familiar to all of us — that of an old man with a beard seated on a throne and surrounded by adoring angels. This image of the Father, painted by the words of the book of Daniel, is really very similar to Michelangelo's great painting on the ceiling of the Sistine Chapel; both can be used as we pray to the Father.

Many people decry such images, calling them childish and unnecessary, but I disagree. As long as they are understood to be what they are — symbols which point to the Father's infinite power, majesty, and wisdom — they are of no danger and can be of some help to us in prayer. In other words, as long as we remember that these images have nothing, literally, to do with the reality of God the Father but only represent this in our minds, they can help us as we address Him or think of Him.

> The Father is not only revealed but made intimate through the love of His Son.

They can also be helpful in a further way. Such images of an older, powerful man remind us of human fathers, and through the understanding of human fatherhood we can glimpse a bit of the Divine Fatherhood. As we attempt to draw near to God the Father, we are greatly aided by Jesus' words in the Gospel and our corresponding images of our Divine Savior praying to His Father or speaking of His Father. It is easier to imagine and relate to the Father when you are in the presence of the Son who loves Him. The Father is not only revealed but made intimate through the love of His Son. Because we have seen other loving sons with loving fathers, it is easier for us to imagine the Father when we are listening to Christ. Jesus' words point to this: "He who has seen me has seen the Father" (John 14:9).

The Holy Spirit, however, presents great problems to us in this area, for we do not have many images or symbols to help us. There are a few found in the Scriptures, of course, but they are difficult to comprehend and even more difficult to relate to. For example, the Spirit is described as descending "like a dove." This occurs in each of the Synoptic Gospels when they speak of the baptism of Jesus in the Jordan by St. John the Baptist. St. Matthew describes it this way:

> And when Jesus was baptized he went up immediately from the water and behold, the heavens were opened and he saw the spirit of God descending like a dove, and alighting on him and lo, a voice from heaven, saying "This is my beloved Son, with whom I am well pleased."
>
> — Matthew 3:17

We also read of the Holy Spirit coming on the feast of Pentecost like a great wind, and then settling over the heads of the apostles as flame.

These are powerful symbols, of course, but they are impersonal — not the kind of images that are likely to be helpful in prayer. We cannot draw near to a dove, or a wind, or a flame in the way we can draw near to the image of Jesus as an itinerant preacher in Palestine, as a worker of miracles, or even as a newborn child in a manger. We certainly cannot do so in the way that we can draw near to Jesus as the suffering servant of God who willingly endures death on the cross for our sake. Thus, we are faced with a problem, an enigma: a Person whom we are unable to envision. However, even this may be slowly changing. As a result of the Charismatic movement, many have become more aware of the mysterious Third Person of The Blessed Trinity. Many realize that the Holy Spirit inspires, guides, strengthens, and counsels us — and that we can be quite aware of the Spirit's presence, even without images, by concentrating on the effects of the Spirit's presence in our lives.

> We can be quite aware of the Spirit's presence, even without images by concentrating on the effects of the Spirit's presence in our lives.

The wind is known by its effects — the sound of the rustling leaves, for example. The Spirit, too, is known by His effects in people's lives. Seeing the effects of the Spirit helps people to draw near to Him and pray to Him, even without concrete images to help us to focus our prayer. In the Gospel of St. John, we read:

"The wind blows where it wills, and you hear the sound of it, but you do not know whence it comes or whither it goes; so it is with every one who is born of the Spirit."

— John 3:8

Meditate on these words and you will begin to better comprehend prayer to the Holy Spirit.

When all is said and done, however, when most Christians cry out to God in times of great difficulty, they probably cry out to Jesus Christ. This is not only because the Second Person of the Blessed Trinity is the easiest for us to imagine but because Christ is our Savior. We are reminded of the words of St. Thomas to Christ: "My Lord and my God!" (John 20:28). Uncountable popular prayers begin with the words "Dear Jesus." These are words addressed to someone with whom we feel intimate, with whom we feel comfortable, at home. By contrast, although many prayers to the Holy Spirit have been composed, I can't think of a single one of them that begins by saying "Dear Holy Spirit," for the Spirit remains too mysterious and unimaginable, too remote to address so intimately. Yet, we can still feel His presence and believe firmly in His love for us.

A BEAUTIFUL PICTURE OF THE HOLY TRINITY

There is a very famous icon of the Holy Trinity, painted in about 1410 by the renowned Russian Orthodox iconographer, St. Andrei Rublev. We keep two copies of this beautiful and mysterious painting at Trinity Retreat, where I have lived for many years — one in the chapel, the other just inside the front door. I make a point of looking at one or the other of these icons every day, because this is an icon that truly invites prayer.

In it, the three members of the Holy Trinity are represented as young men sitting together. Their faces are nearly, but not quite, identical. Each one wears a different blue garment, but the color blue is the same and reminds the viewer of the color of the sky. Each figure has one small distinction in posture or possesses some object that discloses which Person of the Trinity he represents.

For example, the figure that represents the Father sits in front of a house to remind us of Christ's words, "In my Father's house there are many rooms" (John 14:2). This figure sits in great tranquility, wrapped in a shimmering robe that nearly obscures the blue of His inner garment. This suggests to us that the Father is hidden, mysterious. The figure holds a staff that implies the scepter of a ruler.

The figure that represents Christ wears a brown robe, as well as His sky-blue one, to remind us that He took on flesh — the dust of the earth — to save us from sin. He sits before a chalice of red wine — an obvious symbol of the Eucharist and reference to the His blood, outpoured during the Crucifixion.

The figure that represents the Holy Spirit wears a light green robe in addition to His blue one, as if suggesting new life. His hand rests on the table in front of Him, and behind Him is a mountaintop, a place of wild and fierce winds where God was frequently encountered in the Bible.

The Christ figure looks to the Father, and the Spirit's head is inclined toward Christ. The icon is designed in a way that suggests totality, completion, that these three figures form an entire universe, that they need nothing but each other. In this icon we find a powerful image of the Blessed Trinity, perhaps the greatest pictorial representation of the mystery of the Blessed Trinity, of three equal and distinct Persons but one being. I urge all Christians — Western as well as Eastern — to seek out a copy of this icon and gaze at it prayerfully as you meditate on the Holy Trinity.

CHAPTER FOUR

WAYS OF RESPONDING TO GOD

I will extol thee, my God and King,
    and bless thy name for ever and ever,
Every day I will bless thee,
    and praise thy name for ever and ever.

— Psalm 145:1-2

Each of us must ask the same question of ourselves if we are to try to live lives of constant prayer: "What does God mean to me in my everyday life?" We must face this question honestly and unflinchingly, because a great deal depends on our answer. To pray unceasingly we must be aware of the presence of God unceasingly, and we must find the times and places that God especially discloses His presence to us. For each of us these times and places will be different.

> We need the help of some kind of plan, of times specifically set aside for prayer.

A ROUTINE OF PRAYER

A real prayer life in our flesh-and-blood world needs structure. All human endeavors do. In heaven, the holy souls are in a constant, unending prayerful relationship with God. In our earthly lives, even people who are very prayerful by nature will slip into and out of prayer regularly. It is so easy to turn from God to the world, from eternity to an insignificant moment in time. We need the help of some kind of plan, of times specifically set aside for prayer. If we do not take care to do this, our prayer lives will imperceptibly weaken, perhaps even dissipate.

As I am sure everyone knows, we should begin our prayer in the morning, as soon as we awake, and end in the evening, as we go to sleep. We must begin each day by invoking God and asking His blessing for the day, and we must end each day asking His forgiveness for our unavoidable failures and His blessing for the night. These two pillars of the life of prayer — morning and evening prayer — are seen, in one form or another, in most of the religious traditions in the world. They are hallowed by time and tradition.

But what of the rest of the day? It is hoped that most religious people, and certainly most Christians, would be moved at various times during the day to call out to God, to invoke Him. This will not be difficult if we allow the Church to guide us. The Church offers us her "official prayer," the Liturgy of the Hours, also called the Divine Office. In this great prayer, we see the idea of praying regularly throughout the day and praying with the Body of Christ, our voices rising together in chorus, like incense to heaven. While the Liturgy of the Hours is not prayer without cease, it is prayer that we return to over and over again throughout the day — every day — so that we are never far from a moment of prayer.

The Liturgy of the Hours is largely based on psalms and readings from Scripture, structured in such a way that it enables us to turn to God in formal prayer with the Church seven times each day. All priests and religious pray the Liturgy of the Hours, and the laity should pray it as well. It is a profound way to steep our lives in prayer, in the knowledge that the Church herself is praying with us.

But the Liturgy of the Hours is certainly not the only approach we can take to be reminded of regular prayer during the day. The Church offers us many reminders and symbols to help us in this: the ringing of church bells — particularly the Angelus, which calls Catholics to prayer at certain times of the day; the custom of praying before and often after meals; the prayer we make for the ill, for the dying, and particularly when there has been a death. People become especially aware of the need to pray at these times.

BLESSING YOUR DAY

I am reminded of a Jewish custom that I find very beautiful, one that I suspect can be of great help in instilling prayer into daily life.

It is traditional among observant Jews to say a blessing in response to anything good that might happen during the day, no matter how small. For example, you might say a blessing upon waking in the morning, thanking God for bringing you to a new day. A blessing might be said on accidentally meeting a friend whom you have not seen in some time. A blessing might be said on encountering something beautiful in nature, such as a rainbow, a gentle snowfall, or the first spring flowers. In this way, you constantly remind yourself that the little miracles of life are not accidental, that they are gifts of God. Such blessings make one aware of the never-ending presence of God in our lives and in the world around us. In Judaism, these blessings are short and have a standard form: *Blessed are You, Lord our God, Sovereign of the Universe, for _____(whatever you are thankful for — a sunset, a delicious meal, etc.).* It was also traditionally thought that the average number of such blessings each person should say every day was one hundred!

Just think of that. A day in which a person thanks God 100 times is surely a day filled with prayer.

As Christians, why could we not adapt this practice, using our own wording, thanking the Holy Trinity for the many small miracles that attend our lives, but which we usually ignore? Praying 100 times each day may seem a tall order at first; however, such a practice already has a Christian history, as the following quotation taken from the *Confession of St. Patrick* shows:

And as the fear of God increased in me so did my faith, so that in a single day I would pray up to one hundred times and in the course of the night I would pray nearly as many times again. When I was tending the sheep on the mountains and in woods and in the dark before dawn I would awaken and pray in the snow, in the frost and in the rain. No harm came to me as there was no idleness in me, as I can now see, for my spirit was always fervent.[14]

There are certain individuals who find holy, prayerful moments most frequently within the family setting. Usually, they are members of loving Christian families whose homes are sanctuaries of holiness. Their homes — and, by extension their lives — become "dwelling places of prayer."

Others, called to the single life, find that their small homes or apartments become like an oratory, or perhaps even like a Carthusian cell. These are no less intense places of prayer, but the prayer is somewhat different and often more contemplative. I know very devout people who do this well and have been doing it for years.

Still others may become particularly aware of God through His creation, the material world, the sky, the sea, the forest. This can be an extraordinarily powerful experience, one the Irish poet Joseph Mary Plunkett expresses perfectly in the following poem, "I See His Blood upon the Rose."

> I see his blood upon the rose
> And in the stars the glory of his eyes,
> His body gleams amid eternal snows,
> His tears fall from the skies.
> I see his face in every flower;
> The thunder and the singing of the birds
> Are but his voice — and carven by his power
> Rocks are his written words.
> All pathways by his feet are worn,
> His strong heart stirs the ever-beating sea,
> His crown of thorns is twined with every thorn,
> His cross is every tree. [15]

Here, the poet has come to find God — and most especially Christ — revealed in virtually every aspect of nature so that every encounter with the physical world becomes a pathway to prayer, a way of encountering the God who has created all things but is always different from all things.

The person moving in this direction is more and more aware of God's presence, of His creative power pervading all things, the beauty of the material world — of creation — that we perceive in the sky and the sea, and of God's love shown by the presence of animals, particularly pets, which can be a real gift, especially to a lonely person. Finally, there comes the awareness of God as we find Him present in that part of creation He has made in His own image: man. We find a prayerful awareness of God's presence in the good, the blessed, the needy, those who by their troubles call out to us for our pity and concern.

> In those who suffer and in our attempts to aid them, Christ is present in a special way.
> — Prayer at the Foot of the Cross

The profound influence of the passages in the Twenty-fifth Chapter of the Gospel of St. Matthew, concerning the ways in which we find Christ among the hungry and destitute, deserve our prayerful attention — and not just occasionally, but with great regularity. This is a powerful gift given to those who struggle to find God in the most difficult, mysterious, and sometimes appalling parts of life.

Among the greatest gifts Mother Teresa was ever given by God was the ability to perceive Christ in the poor, the ill, and the suffering. This was the start of her work, work that has spread throughout the world. She labored among the poor and the destitute every day of her life, and her sisters continue to do so today. Mother Teresa made the love of God real to those who had often never known love at all. We must admit that this work is holy work — and more. Perhaps it is even a kind of prayer, a prayer reserved by God for a select few.

We hope that prayer will bring us consolation. Often, through the grace of God, it does. Yet sometimes, the opposite happens. We may not like it, but we must accept the fact that prayer will not always be peaceful; it can be disturbing at times. In the religions of Asia — Hinduism and Buddhism, particularly — there is a constant yearning for peace, but a peace that may, at times, seem to be mere tranquility. Surely, we all want tranquility, and there is nothing wrong in that. But for the Christian, tranquility is not all to hope for. The peace of a Christian — the peace of Christ — isn't always tranquil in this world.

The peace of Christ transcends the sufferings of this world, giving meaning to the trials and difficulties of our short lives. We can know the peace of Christ while still acknowledging that we are in the midst of something very real and very difficult, perhaps even terrible. In this world, the peace of Christ is a peace amidst turmoil, a peace amidst the very situations that every human being fears and tries to avoid. The peace of Christ is filled with hope and confidence in God, in the Blessed Trinity. In the peace of Christ we come to know in a very real way that "love is stronger than death." We see this clearly in the following moving words written by the Vietnamese martyr Paul Le-Bao-Tinh and quoted by our Holy Father, Benedict XVI:

> I, Paul, in chains for the name of Christ, wish to relate to you the trials besetting me daily, in order that you may be inflamed with love for God and join with me in his praises, for his mercy is for ever (Ps 136 [135]). The prison here is a true image of everlasting Hell: to cruel tortures of every kind — shackles, iron chains, manacles — are added hatred, vengeance, calumnies,

obscene speech, quarrels, evil acts, swearing, curses, as well as anguish and grief. But the God who once freed the three children from the fiery furnace is with me always; he has delivered me from these tribulations and made them sweet, for his mercy is for ever. In the midst of these torments, which usually terrify others, I am, by the grace of God, full of joy and gladness, because I am not alone — Christ is with me.[16]

The Catholic Christian must understand that our prayer cannot always be tranquil. At times, our prayer may even be anguished, as was Jesus' prayer in the Garden of Gethsemane.

In our time, there is a great risk that we will do what is done in the religions of Asia: that we will use our prayer to withdraw from the world, to act as if the world is not important, an illusion. But it is important, and it is real. In the Gospel of St. John, we are reminded, "God so loved the world that he gave his only Son, that whoever believes in him should not perish but have eternal life" (John 3:16). We all know that Jesus often left His disciples and withdrew to the desert for periods of intense prayer, sometimes for many days at a time. Yet each of these periods of prayer was followed by a return to the world, a return to others and to their concerns. This should be our model; we enter into prayer, at least in part, so that we will be better able to bring Christ to others. If we dare to imitate Jesus in our little ways — to attempt to help the sick, the destitute, and the forgotten — we will encounter Him deeply in these people, and thus find one of the greatest pathways to prayer.

Our society specializes in hiding such people; make no mistake, however: they are there, and they need you.

There are many who are ill and forgotten in our world today. Our society specializes in hiding such people; make no mistake, however: they are there, and they need you. Go to a hospital for the seriously ill. Take a deep breath and go to a hospice, a home for the dying. Visiting the people in such institutions will present us with an important opportunity for prayer — an important opportunity for holiness. In the ill we find Christ, the One we pray to, in a very special way.

The importance of visiting patients who need someone to cheer them up and to pray with them cannot be overestimated. Often, the seriously ill are alone in hospitals and nursing homes. Many of them are sadly ignored by their families and friends — the very people who should be with them constantly. They often spend days, weeks, or even months feeling abandoned, terrifyingly alone, helpless, and hopeless. This is a true crucifixion. As Catholics, we should be well aware that one of the holiest places we can ever stand is at the foot of the cross. I urge you again: go to the ill, to the forgotten, to the abandoned. In them, you will find Christ; in you, they may see the love of Christ, which is something they desperately need to see at this time. It is hard to imagine any more sacred duty for a Christian than visiting and consoling the sick and the dying.

It is, of course, wise to ask if such patients want you to visit or to pray with them, but it has been my experience that most are eager for companionship and the hope that prayer can give. They are desperate to find someone who still sees in them the image of God. They are desperate for someone to hold their hand and listen to them. They are desperate for someone to pray with them or to pray for them, for perhaps they can no longer bring themselves to pray.

All this is difficult to do, and I suggest some spiritual preparation. The infirmity of others points out to us in a very direct way our own fragility. Yet, prayer with the ill can be a source of great grace and an important way to grow in your prayer life and in your spiritual life in general.

In prayer at the foot of the cross, we may come to experience the peace of Christ — and if we are very blessed, we may even be the bearer of that peace amidst turmoil to another.

Responding to God in Silence

Among the most special or cherished experiences of prayer is that of complete silence. Many never know it at all. Some experience it only rarely. Perhaps during a retreat, a person may become aware that God is with him in a special way. This may be partly a function of our own psychology, but that fact does not discount it as a gift of grace. In the lives of the saints we read of this occasionally — those who encounter God in the deep prayer that becomes possible only in silence.

A most profound illustration of this is an experience I had as a young novice many years ago. It is something that has stayed with me for my entire life.

One night I was unable to sleep and decided to go to the chapel to pray for a while. I entered by the side door and knelt in the darkness — only the red glow of the sanctuary lamp provided any light. I tried to pray but suddenly became aware that I was not alone, that there was another presence near me in the chapel. Reaching up and turning on the light, I discovered the Venerable Servant of God, Father

Solanus Casey, deep in prayer, his eyes fixed on the door of the tabernacle. He was completely given over to a kind of prayer that I had never encountered before. I am sure he was absolutely unaware of his surroundings, of me, of anything. For him, at that moment, the universe consisted of nothing but the presence of Christ in the Blessed Sacrament.

I watched in astonishment for a few minutes, aware that he was in ecstasy — a word that means that he was standing outside of himself. Although he was in his eighties by then, and his arms were stretched out in prayer, he didn't move or seem to be uncomfortable in this difficult position. Quickly, I put out the light and retreated to my room, feeling that I had seen something that I had no right to see.

In the course of time I had the opportunity to tell this story as testimony for the canonization process of this most remarkable man, a man of deep prayer, whose intercession has been instrumental in numerous healings and even many events that are called miraculous.

UNEXPECTED ENCOUNTERS WITH GOD

God's presence is often felt and understood by the devout, but occasionally such awareness unexpectedly breaks into the life of a person who may never have even thought of God.[17] A professor of psychology who became a friend of mine in later years, a man who once was my teacher, was utterly removed from religion. Yet, one day as he was passing a bookshop in Manhattan, he happened to notice a Bible on display. Something inside him said very clearly: "There is a better way." He was startled by this thought, but it stayed with him and gradually began to have an effect on him.

He developed a devout, if intellectualized, relationship with God. He never got as far as joining organized Christianity, but certainly by reading and praying and meditating he found God, in his own way, and discovered a kind of fullness in a world that had once seemed terribly empty. It seems to me that it became impossible for this man to return to the bleak world he had once inhabited — such is the grace of God.

> When a person is "surprised by grace," he might find that his first real experiences of prayer are without effort.

For the lifelong Christian, prayer is too often felt as a task or responsibility. Sometimes it is fulfilled with great effort or even with discouragement. On the other hand, when a person is "surprised by grace," he might find that his first real experiences of prayer are without effort and seem to be, themselves, gifts of divine grace. The most dramatic experience of this is that of St. Paul on the road to Damascus, which we read about in the Acts of the Apostles.

But when we have difficulty praying, we need to recall that this is not uncommon, that holy people such as Mother Teresa often had to struggle and work to pray. Prayer is the lifeblood of the spiritual life. Whether it comes to us easily or only after much struggle, it is absolutely necessary for the soul. Without prayer, there can be no real spiritual life.

We must also realize that prayer comes in many forms. Someone may say regretfully, "I cannot pray at all." But this is not entirely true, for those very words are at least the beginning of a prayer, and as he utters them, that person is praying. He has "lifted his heart and soul to God."

Prayer and impulses to prayer are vital in the Christian life, but like so many things, prayer requires practice; it must become (in a good sense) a habit. The reminders to pray we encounter in our daily lives help us in this. They lead us along the way to deeper things, to Sacred Scripture and the teachings the Bible contains, to the presence of God at every place and in every moment of our lives. Such as these are the first steps along the road that leads to what St. Paul calls "praying always."

CHAPTER FIVE

REVERENT WORSHIP
AND ADORATION

Let my prayer be counted as incense before thee,
and the lifting of my hands as an evening sacrifice!

— Psalm 141:2

THE MASS IS THE CORNERSTONE OF
OUR PRAYER LIFE

Most people come to a more frequent experience of daily prayer and an awareness of God's presence supported by the prayers of the Church, especially by the holy Sacrifice of the Mass. We have already discussed the fact that a person who wishes to pray frequently should begin each day with some kind of personal formal prayer. While this is absolutely essential, we should never think that it is enough, for no kind of prayer can ever substitute for the Holy Eucharist. The Fathers of the Second Vatican Council said the following about the importance of the Eucharistic Sacrifice:

> Taking part in the Eucharistic sacrifice, the source and
> summit of the Christian life, [the faithful] offer the divine
> victim to God and themselves along with it. And so it is

that, both in the offering and in Holy Communion, each in his own way, though not of course indiscriminately, has his own part to play in the liturgical action. Then, strengthened by the body of Christ in the Eucharistic communion, [the faithful] manifest in a concrete way that unity of the People of God which this holy sacrament aptly signifies and admirably realizes.[18]

If prayer is an encounter with the living God, then clearly the Mass, in which we encounter Jesus Christ in a unique way that cannot be surpassed in this life, must be of the utmost importance.

I once heard someone say that "in the Mass, heaven and earth kiss."

Often we have busy schedules and may be tempted to rush, but we must remember that the Mass is something that should never be rushed. We must always approach the Mass with the greatest reverence and love, remembering that in the Mass, heaven and earth meet. I once heard someone say that "in the Mass, heaven and earth kiss." This is a somewhat sentimental way of expressing things, but it is nonetheless a startling way of indicating the reality of the Mass.

We see this meeting, this "kissing," shown clearly in a few lines from the First Eucharistic Prayer (the Roman Canon), in which the priest prays for God's angel to take our sacrifice to His "altar in heaven," from which we will in turn receive the body and blood of His Son.

Think of the imagery in these lines: heaven, in the form of an angel, stoops down to our sinful, dying world, exchanging our poor sacrifice for the one sacrifice that brings us redemption and new life. If we truly understood the Mass in such terms, how could we not approach it prayerfully?

It is vital that we prepare ourselves mentally and spiritually by arriving before Mass, collecting our thoughts, and immersing ourselves in prayer. This is a time for leaving the cares and distractions of the world behind, for making sure that we do not go to meet Jesus either casually or unprepared. While we are participating in the Mass, we should tolerate no distractions but focus all our attention on the Liturgy. After Mass, we should not rush away but stay for a while to make a good thanksgiving and to speak personally to Christ.

APPROACHING THE LITURGY WITH PRAYER AND REVERENCE

The very first thing we must have in order to be prayerful and reverent during Mass is a fairly good understanding of the Liturgy and its meaning for the world and the individual. Many people today do not understand what the Mass is, and therefore cannot really appreciate it in any way. Innumerable books have been written about the liturgy over the years, and there are many good ones you can obtain.[19]

Without any hesitation, I urge you to learn directly from the Church Herself regarding prayer and the liturgy. If you are inclined to read papal documents, the monumental teaching, *Mystici Corpus Christi* (*On the Mystical Body of Christ*) by Pope Pius XII, is a wonderful place to begin. It is available on the Internet and in book form. I cannot praise it highly enough. Also easily obtainable are the very good sections regarding the Mass in the *Catechism of the Catholic Church*. Apparently, Cardinal Schönborn of Vienna did most of this writing, and it is excellent. No Catholic should be without a copy of the *Catechism*.

UNDERSTANDING IS VITAL, BUT SO IS REVERENCE

Some years ago when I was in Japan, I went to Kyoto, the sacred city of the Shinto religion. I was looking at the beautiful mahogany and ivory statues of various religious figures that were kept in several chapels there. In those chapels, I saw people being devout and prayerful. I stopped in a small temple where a young Shinto priest was engaged in the liturgical prayer of this religion. It was remarkable to see that he did everything quite precisely and reverently. It was, without a doubt, the wrong prayer in the right way. I say the "wrong prayer" because the Shinto religion has no theological content at all. Literally, a Shinto does not know what he's doing or why he's doing it. He does, however, know that he's doing something devout and reverent to the mysterious power that sustains the universe.

Unfortunately we find that many Catholics do the right prayer in the wrong way. They seem to have at least a basic theological knowledge of the Mass, which is good, but they — unlike the Shinto priest — are sadly short on reverence and prayerfulness; too bad!

If you want to be a devout and prayerful member of the Church, be a good example and invite others to pray. Encourage devout liturgy. Those clergy and seminarians reading this book must accept the responsibility that is theirs. It is their task to make of the Mass a truly prayerful experience for everyone present. More than once, I have heard a priest in his old age express regret that he had not approached the Mass more devoutly; this is a sad admission.

PRAYER BEFORE THE BLESSED SACRAMENT

If you have begun your day with Mass, you have begun the best way. The Mass will prepare you and strengthen you to live your life every day as a true Catholic Christian. It will enable you to better confront the inevitable temptations of life. Fortified by the Eucharist, you will find that your heart and soul turn to prayer more easily and more often. In a very real sense, the Mass is the cornerstone of the Catholic's prayer life, the source from which everything else flows.

> You must never take it for granted that by attending Mass you have done enough, because when it comes to prayer we can literally never do enough.

But you must not stop at the Mass. You must never take it for granted that by attending Mass you have done enough, because when it comes to prayer we can literally never do enough. You should always be very conscious of what you are doing as you make your way through the day. And you must strive always to be aware of those simple events that call upon you to pray: getting into a car, stopping to eat a meal, walking quietly in the street, stepping into a church for a moment, stopping to give some money to a homeless man begging on the sidewalk. You must pause at these times, make yourself aware of the constant presence and love of God, and offer our Heavenly Father whatever kind of prayer you are capable of at that particular moment. It may not be profound — that's not really important — but it must be sincere. All of these events and countless more can open our minds and hearts to God if we allow them to. They are all gates of prayer, we have but to open them.

Certainly for a Catholic, frequent adoration of Christ in the Blessed Sacrament is essential — particularly if one is fortunate enough to live in an area in which churches are not locked during the day. It is quite surprising in a busy city like New York to find that most mid-town churches are often filled with people coming to pray quietly before the Blessed Sacrament, some for long periods of time, some for only a moment or two. It is a revelation to the average person to discover that so many churches in New York and other large cities are regularly open for prayer and meditation, for the silence of prayer amid the constant noise of the city. In fact, several churches in New York are open all day long. St. Patrick's Cathedral alone will see about 7,000 people during an ordinary day. Many of these are just tourists, of course; however, large numbers do pause to pray, and many go to the Lady Chapel, in which the Blessed Sacrament is exposed. An atmosphere of prayer and silence pervades that whole part of the Cathedral.

For some years after the Second Vatican Council, prayer before the Blessed Sacrament seemed to be on the decline. I am very pleased to tell you that this is no longer the case, and now many churches have regular hours of adoration. Some large parishes even manage to have adoration for twenty-four hours a day during one or more days each week.

Many people have asked me what is important about prayer before the Blessed Sacrament, what makes it different from other types of prayer. The answer to those questions could fill volumes with dense theological writing. I believe that for anyone firmly grounded in the Catholic faith, however, no reasons or explanations for prayer before the Blessed Sacrament need be given. It is self-explanatory. Prayer before the Blessed Sacrament is prayer before the sacramental presence of Christ. When we kneel prayerfully before the Blessed Sacrament, we kneel before the Divine Presence in a way that can only be surpassed by the Mass itself. Father John Hardon, a wonderful Jesuit writer whose works have helped strengthen the faith of many, wrote:

> One of the best ways to look at prayer before the Blessed Sacrament is to see it as an extension of Holy Communion. Christ Himself could not have been plainer when He called Himself "the Bread of Life" and told us to eat His Body and drink His Blood. What we may overlook, however, is that the spiritual nourishment that comes from the Eucharist does not end with Holy Communion. Of course, there is an efficacy that comes from the actual reception of the Sacrament that is special and distinctive, but we are not talking about that now. There is also a nourishment that takes place in what we may casually call "spiritual communion." How cheap the phrase sounds! But it is neither casual nor cheap. It is profoundly meaningful. As we pray before the Blessed Sacrament our souls are fed by the Person of the Savior in the two faculties of spirit that need to be constantly fed. They are the mind and the will. In the mind we need light; in the will we need strength. And both needs are met in an extraordinary way through earnest prayer before the Eucharist. Remember, we said it is still the Blessed Sacrament. It is not the residue of the Sacrament. It is not the remnants

after the Sacrament. It is not a memory of the Blessed Sacrament. It is the Blessed Sacrament.[20]

ST. FRANCIS OF ASSISI AND EUCHARISTIC ADORATION

People are usually surprised to learn that devotion to Christ's presence in the Eucharist outside of the liturgy is only about 800 years old. Adoration of the Blessed Sacrament is a gift of God that comes to us very much through St. Francis of Assisi. Francis, profoundly conscious of the presence of Christ in the Eucharist, regularly did the rather unusual thing of praying to Christ near the place where the consecrated Host was kept for people who were sick or dying. Usually, the Eucharist was preserved in a cupboard in the sacristy or sometimes, more solemnly, in a metal image of a dove over the altar or in the side of the sanctuary.

St. Francis wrote three letters to different groups of people regarding adoration and safe care of the Holy Eucharist: one letter to bishops and priests, one to his friars, and one to government officials, including princes. In these letters, St. Francis encouraged people to show great devotion to the Eucharist and to reserve the Body of Christ with the utmost care.

As soon as St. Francis began devotion to the Eucharistic presence, it spread like wildfire. In only a generation or two, such devotion had become established throughout Europe — a remarkable fact when we consider that this was long before the days of rapid communication and easy travel.

About 100 years later, through the mystic Blessed Juliana of Mt. Cornillon, the Feast of *Corpus Christi* was established by Pope Urban IV.[21] From that day until this, devotion to Christ's presence in the Eucharist and the reservation of the Eucharist in a place of honor has been an important and vibrant part of Catholic tradition.

In the National Shrine of the Immaculate Conception, high around the altar, one will find seven or eight statues of saints shown in their devotion to the Eucharist. Included is the Franciscan brother St. Pascal Baylon; St. John Vianney; St. Pierre Eymard, founder of the Blessed Sacrament Fathers; and even my own humble patron, St. Benedict Joseph Labré, the troubled, homeless man who spent most of his life praying before the Eucharist and was known in Rome as the "man of the forty hours" because he was seen in parish after parish whenever the Eucharist was exposed for this devotion.

Praying to Christ in the Eucharist can be a very personal experience. It is an experience of reverence, silence, and prayerful devotion that uses either your own words or some of the many prayers composed to Christ in the Eucharist. If you have never developed devotion to Christ in the Eucharist, then your prayer life, no matter how deep it is, is lacking something important. Today is the day that you should begin.

Go to a church; kneel before the tabernacle and pray to Christ — who is only a few feet away from you! Become aware that when you are in the Eucharistic Presence of Christ, you have truly entered the Holy of Holies. Offer yourself to Him; listen to Him; rejoice in the fact that He loves you and comes to you in this remarkable way. I know even a few Protestant people who pray quietly before the Eucharist in Catholic churches. They have come to understand something of what the Eucharist means. Surely, every Catholic should do no less.

CHAPTER SIX

SACRED PLACES OF PRAYER

I shall dwell in the house of the Lord as long as I live.

— Psalm 23:6

In our time, we often hear people speak of "sacred space." These words have almost become a cliché, but we should never dismiss this concept, for it is very real. In certain places it is far easier to feel the presence of God, far easier to pray, than in others.

PLACES WHERE GOD DWELLS

Shortly after I visited Russia during the final days of Communist domination, on the feast of the Assumption of the Blessed Virgin, I had the wonderful opportunity to visit several of the churches that are part of the Kremlin. (In the East, they call this feast the "Dormition" — the falling to sleep — of the Blessed Virgin.) As I recall, there were seven churches there, and another one across the street, which was named Our Lady of Vladimir. That ancient church, honoring a miraculous icon, had been almost destroyed and had been rebuilt only shortly before I was there. The other churches in the Kremlin had removed all the anti-religious signs and paraphernalia that had defaced them for so long.

There was not yet any sign of liturgical appointments, but the churches were clean and orderly. I noticed that when a man tried to walk behind the iconostasis (the partition decorated with icons that separates the nave of an eastern church from the sanctuary) he was stopped by a guard and told that only a priest was permitted to do that. Communism was certainly on its way out, and faith was on its way back.

I was being shadowed by a secret agent, whom I made no attempt to escape. In fact, when I returned to the American embassy, I waved back to him in a friendly way.

I spent some time praying in each of these churches for the Christianization of Russia and for the end of the Soviet empire. It was a profoundly spiritual experience. Over and over again, I recited the Rosary in the different churches, each of which had a beautiful name: the Dormition, Holy Apostles, the Holy Shroud, the Annunciation. I felt assisted in prayer by the inspiration of the Holy Spirit, who seemed to me to be very real in these places. It was clear that these churches, which had been unused for years and desecrated by the communists, had not truly been changed. They were still churches. One would have to be incredibly insensitive not to notice that they were, in fact, "sacred space," special places conducive to prayer. (I did notice that I was being shadowed by a secret agent, whom I made no attempt to escape. In fact, when I returned to the American embassy, I waved back to him in a friendly way, indicating that I hoped he had enjoyed visiting seven churches. I have always hoped that our day of prayer and pilgrimage meant something to him.)

The idea of sacred space, so often abused in our time, is not only a very Orthodox one; it is also a very Catholic idea. If we want to pray deeply and well, we would be wise to pay attention to it. We have already spoken of the way in which the Eucharistic Presence transforms a mere building into a holy place, a "tabernacle of prayer."

SACRED SPACE AND OUR SENSES

There is yet another way in which the space around us can influence our prayer: through the senses.

We should recall that for the Catholic, prayer must not be thought of as something entirely limited to the mind or even to the soul. Prayer can, and should, involve every bit of us, our bodies as well as our minds, our senses as well as our souls. Catholic prayer — both liturgical and non-liturgical — has always been marked by this. Beautiful vestments, processions, and liturgical gestures appeal to our sense of sight, as do statues, icons, and stained glass windows. Appropriate music, especially Gregorian chant, can be very powerful in its ability to draw us into deep prayer though sound. We stand, kneel, genuflect, and bow in a choreography of prayer during the Mass, making our reverence visible though the movement of our bodies. We hold rosaries, letting the smooth beads slip between our fingers as we pray. Even our sense of smell can be involved with our prayer, the scent of incense or that of beeswax candles reminding us that the very air around us is pervaded with God's holiness, with the presence of Christ.

> Prayer can and should involve every bit of us, our bodies as well as our minds, our senses as well as our souls.

Some Protestants are suspicious of such practices, imagining they find in them more than a hint of idolatry or superstition. This is a great misunderstanding, and Catholics should not make this mistake. God has given us His magnificent creation and His constant presence. This is the reason we should not always withdraw completely within ourselves to pray. At least at times, we should let the very space around us be a constant reminder of the beauty of God's love for us. We are not disembodied spirits like the angels. God has made us to be physical beings, and He has placed us in a physical world, in a world we touch, and see, and hear. Our prayer, therefore, must be the prayer of flesh-and-blood creatures.

Perhaps you might find a church or a chapel somewhere near your home in which you feel especially peaceful and serene. Try to find one that seems to you to be suffused with the presence of God. Make this place one of your spiritual homes. Return to it regularly for prayer, for meditation — for just a few moments away from the commotion of the world. Such surroundings will have an effect on you over time. They will help you to make prayer more real, more profound.

REDISCOVERING SHRINES

Visiting a shrine can also enhance your prayer experience. Shrines were an extraordinarily important part of Catholic piety in the past, significant in the spiritual development of many people. Unfortunately, in the '70s and '80s, we forgot much of their meaning. But this can be rediscovered: it is there waiting for you, as it was there waiting for me in the churches in the Kremlin.

I live in New York state, where we have a magnificent shrine at Auriesville, about a three-hour drive northwest of New York City. At Auriesville (or very near it), St. Isaac Jogues and his companions, St. René Goupil and St. Jean de Lalande, French Jesuit missionaries, were martyred by the Mohawks during the 1640s. Their great sacrifice for the faith, as well as the blood they spilled on this land, make Auriesville Shrine truly holy ground, genuine sacred space.

Many years ago, Catholics from all over came to Auriesville to pray. They came by the busload. People from New York, Boston, and Montreal — from which Auriesville is more or less equidistant — were there in large numbers all through the warm months when this shrine was open to the public. A thriving retreat house, on the splendid grounds of this shrine, was always full of priests as well as lay people. These days, however, Auriesville Shrine seems a sadly forgotten place, a place people pass on their way to somewhere else. Many other shrines have suffered the same sad fate — but fortunately, this situation can change.

I urge you to make a pilgrimage to Auriesville or to some other shrine. And make sure it is a pilgrimage, not merely a trip. Make prayer the true reason for your being there. Focus your attention on whatever the message of that particular shrine may be. At Auriesville, it is the North American Martyrs, but other shrines are devoted to our Lady, a saint, or, perhaps, to a mystery in the life of Christ. Let the shrine's message linger with you even after you have gone. Find a way to incorporate its message deeply into your life so that even after you have left the shrine, it will still be with you. Let such a shrine become a place of regular personal pilgrimage for you. If you cannot find a place like that, or if you live too far from a shrine, then go to the cathedral of your diocese or an impressive church in your town and pray there.

> We all have the power to create sacred space in our lives.

Sacred space is not limited to churches and shrines: we all have the power to create sacred space in our lives. Of course, this sacred space is not equivalent to a church or chapel where the Blessed Sacrament is reserved, but you'll find it's often possible to turn a corner of your home into a quiet, out-of-the-way space in which you might focus your attention on some sacred object such as a crucifix or an icon. There are many ways of achieving a sense of sacred space, and sacred space need not be a very large space. I once met a woman who prayed every day in the same chair by the same window in her home. As she did so, she wrapped herself in an old shawl (she called it her prayer shawl) — thus symbolically shutting out the world to be alone with God. She had found all the sacred space she needed, even though it was only the space immediately surrounding her body.

CHAPTER SEVEN

GROWING DEEPER IN PRAYER

Come to him, to that living stone, rejected by men but in God's sight chosen and precious; and like living stones be yourselves built into a spiritual house, to be a holy priesthood, to offer spiritual sacrifices acceptable to God through Jesus Christ.

— 1 Peter 2:4-5

The deeper kind of prayer that we yearn for causes a person to look quietly into his soul, to step away from the distractions of the moment, perhaps to close his eyes and kneel, to turn away from the noise that constantly surrounds us. This is not a rejection of life but a sharpening of life, a turning of life to the right direction. Experienced "pray-ers" pray often, they pray well, and they pray deeply. Sometimes they stop to pray, but often they are in the midst of prayer as they accomplish the tasks of daily life. They may not have a lot of time, but they understand that wherever they are and whatever they are doing they are in God's presence. This enables them to use their time well, to be always close to a moment of prayer.

DEVELOPING YOUR PRACTICE OF PRAYER

Look into yourself and see how you pray. Is prayer a natural part of your life as you walk down the street or wait in line at the supermarket, or is it something you must remind yourself constantly to do? When you are in some very public place, surrounded by people, do you occasionally have a sense of solitude, of peace, of being in the holy presence of God?

Think about your day. Is your mind always racing, always given over to the minutiae of daily life, the trivial things that occupy the thoughts of so many — or do you find your thoughts turning to God as the needle of a magnet turns to the north? How often do you pause, even for a few moments, to thank God, to speak to God, to implore God, or simply to acknowledge the presence of God? How often do you look around yourself and see the world as God's creation, rather than as just a collection of things to use?

> How often do you look around yourself and see the world as God's creation, rather than as just a collection of things to use?

A life of prayer will not develop without some effort. Try to organize your life in such a way that certain days can give you the opportunity to pray more intensely than usual and for longer periods. This may mean that you should schedule a retreat or consider making a pilgrimage. It may simply mean that on a certain day you will make a point to visit a church or shrine to pray the Rosary before the Blessed Sacrament. As we try to deepen our prayer lives, it's important to spend some time doing such things. Although they may seem small, little by little, they will help you infuse prayer more deeply into your life.

THE CHURCH OFFERS US MANY OPPORTUNITIES FOR PRAYER

Prayer can be very spontaneous, and such prayer can be extraordinarily satisfying, but we can never count on such spontaneity; it is rare in anyone's life, even the lives of great saints. As we have already noted, anyone who wishes to advance in the life of prayer must develop a daily routine of prayer — one that is tailored to his needs and works specifically for him, one that depends to some extent on praying at specific times during the day. This is the sort of thing that should constantly evolve through your life. It shouldn't be static over long periods of time but should be adapted as your needs change and as your spiritual life matures.

In establishing such a routine, we should construct for ourselves a daily schedule of prayer, what is often called a *horarium*. Strangely enough, as people become more advanced in the life of prayer, they often (although not always) need less structure: their prayer becomes simpler and simpler. It is often less-experienced people who need a rather intricate horarium and many different types of prayers. Nonetheless, I cannot stress strongly enough that, for every Catholic, the cornerstone of this must be participation in daily Mass whenever possible. As we have discussed, our entire prayer life must be anchored in the Mass, which is the greatest of all possible prayers. Yet the Mass alone is not enough. We must be very careful to take advantage of the times for prayer that we've set aside, even (sometimes, especially) if we do not feel in a particularly prayerful mood when they roll around.

The old custom of the Angelus was well suited to this. Church bells would remind the faithful at six in the morning, at noon, and then again at six in the evening to pause, put aside the normal things of life, and enter a brief time of prayer. Such bells are rarely rung these days, but that doesn't mean that we can't stop at those traditional times and pray the Angelus, making it an important part of our routine of prayer.

THE HOLY HOUR

If the times of the Angelus don't suit you, for whatever reason, why not think of stopping in a church at a regular time each day — perhaps in the evening before it closes — for a few moments of prayer? Or, perhaps you could spend an hour before the Eucharistic Presence of Christ in the Blessed Sacrament. This is called a holy hour, and it has been part of the practice of innumerable saints and great Catholics for many centuries. If you let it, it can become one of the most powerful experiences of your life. Mother Teresa gave the friars and sisters of our community this advice, recommending a daily holy hour for each one of us. We have always followed this wise advice, to great benefit.

I remember that it was Mother Teresa's invariable custom to make such a holy hour every day at four o'clock in the morning and then again at four o'clock in the afternoon. That is a remarkable — and strenuous — program of prayer for an elderly person not in good health, but she did it without fail.

Archbishop Fulton J. Sheen never permitted a day to pass without his spending a full hour in prayer before the Blessed Sacrament.

Archbishop Fulton J. Sheen also started each day with a holy hour. A man of many talents, he was also a very busy man. He had a very successful weekly television show; he was a very sought-after speaker and involved in a thousand other tasks. Yet he never permitted a day to pass without his spending a full hour in prayer before the Blessed Sacrament.

One story told about him concerns an incident that occurred toward the end of the archbishop's life, during the first trip of Pope John Paul II to the United States. Everyone was in St. Patrick's Cathedral to welcome the new pope — everyone *except* Archbishop Sheen, that is. The archbishop was eventually found in an out-of-the-way chapel, lost in prayer before the Eucharistic Presence of Christ. Perhaps some of the other clergy were a bit embarrassed, but the pope himself understood completely and fully approved of Archbishop Sheen's brief absence. In fact, when the pope greeted Archbishop Sheen, he said: "You have written and spoken well of the Lord Jesus Christ. You are a loyal son of the Church."

THE LITURGY OF THE HOURS: THE OFFICIAL PRAYER OF THE CHURCH

Certain practices may be helpful to certain individuals but not to others. Certain practices may be helpful to someone at one point in his life but not at other points. Prayer, since it is a relationship, is a very individual thing. Each of us is different; each of us has individual needs; each of us speaks to God out of our unique individuality; each of us hears the voice of God as no one else ever has or ever will. Nonetheless, there are practices that have withstood the test of time, that have proved beneficial for countless people. The Liturgy of the Hours is one of them.

This great cycle of prayer draws deeply on a wealth of Sacred Scripture, as well as the writings of the Church Fathers. Many Catholics find it daunting when they begin to pray the Hours, but this should not be so. The Liturgy of the Hours can be tailored to suit the needs of even the busiest person among us. It is certainly not necessary to say each office during the day, and it is easy to find a version that presents the Liturgy of the Hours in a shortened or simplified form.[22] Perhaps you might obtain such a version and start with Morning and Evening Prayer. Eventually, you might add Night Prayer, just before you go to bed in the evening. This would probably take a total of only twenty minutes during the day, but its benefits are many. It is a way of sanctifying time, and the psalms, of which most of the Liturgy of the Hours is comprised, connect us with untold generations of Christians and Jews who have found great spiritual meaning in these ancient prayers.

THE ROSARY: ONE OF THE CHURCH'S GREAT TREASURES

This brings us to one of the great and most famous prayers of Catholicism: the Holy Rosary, the importance of which has been confirmed by many popes, as well as by numerous private revelations. St. Bernadette and other visionaries have seen the Blessed Virgin holding the Rosary, as if offering it to them in prayer. It is interesting to note that the Blessed Mother herself is never seen to be *praying* the Rosary in these visions. Nonetheless, the Holy Rosary is the prayer that is most connected in the Catholic mind with our Lady, and with very good reason.

In his beautiful papal letter *Rosarium Virginis Mariae*, Pope John Paul II said:

> The Rosary, though clearly Marian in character, is at heart a Christocentric prayer. In the sobriety of its elements, it has all the depth of the Gospel message in its entirety, of which it can be said to be a compendium. It is an echo of the prayer of Mary, her perennial Magnificat for the work of the redemptive Incarnation which began in her virginal womb. With the Rosary, the Christian people sits at the school of Mary and is led to contemplate the beauty on the face of Christ and to experience the depths of his love. Through the Rosary the faithful receive abundant grace, as though from the very hands of the Mother of the Redeemer.[23]

The word *rosary* actually means "a rose garden," but it can also mean a circle of roses. This indicates that the Rosary is meant to become like a secluded place of prayer for us, an oasis of prayer within our busy lives, a place where we can put aside our distractions and focus on the mysteries of Christ and His mother. Envision yourself in the midst of such a rose garden, one provided for you by Jesus and Mary; take advantage of this gift of a special place of prayer which they give to you. Certainly, through the private revelations of the Blessed Mother, she has repeatedly requested that people offer the beautiful prayer of the Rosary.

The Rosary comforts us when we are worried and reassures us when we are distressed.

The Rosary can be prayed at almost any time: when we are resting, when we are walking, when we are sitting quietly in a church. The Rosary comforts us when we are worried and reassures us when we are distressed. As we say its familiar prayers, we feel ourselves to be in the company of our Blessed Mother; we feel her love for us and for her divine Son. The constant repetition of well-known prayers — ten Hail Marys, followed over and over again by an Our Father — help us to allow our minds to concentrate on the events through which God brought about our salvation.

In the Joyful Mysteries, the Luminous Mysteries (which were only recently given to us by Pope John Paul II), the Sorrowful Mysteries, and the Glorious Mysteries, we are allowed to enter into the life of Jesus, brought into His life by Mary. As we pray the Rosary, for a brief moment we experience those events in our own souls, starting with the Annunciation, the Visitation, and the Nativity of our Lord and going all the way through to His Crucifixion and death, His Resurrection from the dead and Ascension. Finally, we see His great love for humankind made manifest in His love for His Mother. In awe we contemplate the love that caused Him to bring her to heaven, body and soul, in the Assumption; and we rejoice at God's declaration of Mary, our humble and loving Mother, as Queen of Heaven and Earth.

In certain ways, the Holy Rosary can historically be linked to the Liturgy of the Hours. In early times, the Liturgy of the Hours was necessarily restricted primarily to monks and nuns, who were among the few who could read. They prayed the entire Psalter (Biblical Book of Psalms) of 150 psalms each week. Ordinary laity certainly had no means to do this, so 150 Hail Marys became their substitute. Records of this going back as far as the second century A.D. reveal that often, a knotted cord was used to keep track of these prayers. Thus, from a yearning to pray the Liturgy of the Hours was born the first Rosaries, showing the connection between all valid forms of prayer.

It's interesting to note that the use of beads as an aid in prayer is not limited to Catholic devotion but is common throughout the world. In 1918, the Reverend S. C. Hughson, a member of an Anglican religious order called the Order of the Holy Cross, noted:

> Almost any encyclopædia will inform the reader that the use of beads in prayer is far older than Christianity itself and belongs to almost every race which has any highly developed system of prayer.

> It will be a surprise to many, no doubt, to know that our common English word bead is derived from the Saxon word bid, to pray, the derivation arising from the fact that our ancestors made common use of perforated pebbles, or beads, upon which to count their prayers. It will be news even to most Catholics to learn that instead of their Rosaries being spoken of as beads because of a resemblance to the common ornament of the name, the ornament takes its name from the Rosary.[24]

A POWERFUL CONTEMPORARY USE OF THE ROSARY: THE DIVINE MERCY CHAPLET

Few Catholics of our time are completely unaware of the private revelations given to St. Faustina. Her diary has been read by large numbers of people. In virtually every Catholic church throughout the world hangs a picture of Christ with rays of light streaming from His heart; this is St. Faustina's vision of Christ as the Divine Mercy. The Sunday after Easter was named by Pope John Paul II as Divine Mercy Sunday. Rarely in the history of the Church has one devotion become so popular and so powerful.

At the very heart of Faustina's spirituality lies the Divine Mercy Chaplet, a series of prayers that make use of Rosary beads. It is usually prayed at 3:00 P.M., the time that Christ died on the cross. The Divine Mercy Chaplet repeats prayers, as does the traditional Rosary. For example, the following words are said on the same beads one would use to say the Our Father during the traditional Rosary: "Eternal Father, I offer You the Body and Blood, Soul and Divinity of Your dearly beloved Son, Our Lord Jesus Christ, in atonement for our sins and those of the whole world." Then, on the ten beads that one would use to say the Hail Mary, one would say, "For the sake of His sorrowful Passion, have mercy on us and on the whole world."

The Divine Mercy Chaplet can be an enormous help in deepening the prayer of many. Our Lord promised particular graces when this is prayed in the presence of the dying. It also shows the flexibility inherent in the use of the Rosary.

THE JESUS PRAYER

In a book that deals with praying without cease, we could certainly not omit some discussion of the Jesus Prayer, because the whole purpose of this ancient Eastern prayer is exactly that: to enable the Christian to pray constantly. The Jesus Prayer is simple, consisting of only a few words: "Lord Jesus Christ, Son of God, have mercy on me, a sinner." This prayer comes to us originally from *hesychasm*, a specific form of quietude in the Orthodox Church. *Hesychasm* was centered on the Jesus Prayer — at times to the exclusion of other forms of prayer.

The Jesus Prayer, often prayed on Rosary beads or on a knotted leather belt, is deceptively simple but can become very deep if we let it. In the Orthodox Church, it is very revered — people generally only begin to make it part of their spiritual lives while being guided by a competent spiritual director. Bishop Kallistos (Timothy) Ware, who has written widely on Orthodox spirituality, has this to say about the Jesus Prayer:

> The Jesus Prayer is a prayer of marvelous versatility. It is a prayer for beginners but equally a prayer that leads to the deepest mysteries of the contemplative life.[25]

The way to pray the Jesus Prayer is very clear: First, one repeats the prayer a number of times in a soft whisper. It is important to do this in an atmosphere of silence and solitude. Then, one slowly stops uttering the prayer but continues to repeat it silently in the mind. One keeps repeating it in this way as long as is possible. If one is forced to stop for some reason, one begins again as soon as possible.

The goal of praying the Jesus Prayer is to eventually incorporate it into one's biorhythms. It should become linked with the beating of the heart. Bishop Ware tells us:

> For some there comes a time when the Jesus Prayer
> enters into the heart, so that it is no longer recited by
> a deliberate effort, but recites itself spontaneously,
> continuing even when a man walks or writes, present
> in his dreams, waking him up in the morning.[26]

This is obviously prayer that is truly constant.

Some people have thought that the Jesus Prayer was similar to the meditative practices one finds in Asian religions. This misses the point. Orthodox Bishop Ignatius Brianchaninov explains the difference:

> The Eastern Church has most often sought to obey the
> commandment to "pray without ceasing" through the
> unceasing use of the Jesus Prayer: Lord, Jesus Christ,
> Son of God, have mercy on me, a sinner. The quiet
> repetition of this prayer is not an effort at the creation
> of a Christian mantra — but rather a way of remaining
> present to God in a state of repentance.[27]

And Bishop Ware tells us, "Those brought up in the tradition of the Jesus Prayer are never allowed for one moment to forget the Incarnate Christ."[28]

The Jesus Prayer can be a great challenge to us as we strive to pray constantly. Born in the solitude of Eastern monasteries, it can sometimes seem ill-suited to our contemporary life. But it has brought great spiritual depth to many in both the West and the East, and it has probably truly brought some people to prayer without cease.

Novenas, based on the Latin word for nine, remind us of the nine days between Ascension Thursday and Pentecost Sunday, days that the apostles devoted themselves entirely to intense prayer.

SIMPLE PRAYERS CAN BE PROFOUND

Novenas, based on the Latin word for *nine*, remind us of the nine days between Ascension Thursday and Pentecost Sunday, days that the apostles devoted themselves entirely to intense prayer. There are innumerable novenas that have been composed over the centuries to imitate — or, rather, emulate this. Each of us is aware of at least some of them. This form of prayer, too, has fallen on hard times in recent years, with fewer and fewer Catholics taking advantage of it. But novenas have for centuries been a means by which Catholics have been able to enter into prayer. We can easily turn to them again, as did our fathers and our mothers.

We should never disparage traditional forms of prayer. We must never assume that the popular devotions of years ago have become meaningless, when the problem is simply that we now fail to find the meaning in them.

One of the holiest people I ever met, the Servant of God Terence Cardinal Cooke, often used such prayers and devotions. His spirituality, which was strong and deep, was based primarily on the religion of his Irish forebears, the prayers that have been used for untold generations. He included many such prayers in the only prayer book he ever wrote, *Prayers for Today*, called by many "The Little Red Prayer Book." I highly recommend this book. Its simplicity conceals a great depth — the depth that is always contained in the prayers people have used for centuries.

St. Peter says that we should come to Jesus as the cornerstone and be built into spiritual houses of prayer. And the Church gives us building blocks like the Liturgy of the Hours, the Rosary, the Divine Mercy Chaplet, the

Jesus Prayer, and practices like novenas to help us construct a pattern of prayer that will draw us close to God.

CHAPTER EIGHT

PRAYING WITH SCRIPTURE

> Ever since you were a child you have known the holy scriptures — from these you can learn the wisdom that leads to salvation through faith in Christ Jesus. All scripture is inspired by God and can profitably be used for teaching, for refuting error and for guiding people's lives and teaching them to be holy.
>
> — 2 Timothy 3:16

In my book *Listening at Prayer,* I have already outlined the steps involved in praying with the Scriptures. Now I want to help you find ways to bring the Holy Scriptures into your prayer life on a regular basis.

When you pick up a copy of the Holy Bible, it looks and feels more or less like any other book. Contemporary copies of the Bible that are bound in paper may even seem to be exactly like every other book on your shelf. In the past, however, the printing of the Bible was given special attention. It was rare to see a copy of the Scriptures that did not have golden edges and a leather cover. The gold and leather alerted you to the fact that you were holding a special book, but that was not entirely the truth: you were holding *the* special book.

When we read
Holy Scripture,
we are reading
a book like
no other.

Of course, we can't tell simply by looking at a Bible or holding one in our hands in what profound way it is different from other books. But we must be constantly aware that, when we read Holy Scripture, we are reading a book like no other. We must be aware of its uniqueness and its great difference from all other books; we must always keep in mind the fact that the Bible contains not just the words of men but the Holy Word of God. The author of the letter to the Hebrews tells us:

> For the word of God is living and active, sharper than any two-edged sword, piercing to the division of soul and spirit, of joints and marrow, and discerning the thoughts and intentions of the heart.
>
> — Hebrews 4:12

THE WORD OF GOD IN THE WORDS OF MEN

Various scholars throughout the ages — Jewish and Christian alike — up to the present moment, understand the idea of "the word of God" in the Bible differently, but they all agree that this is what sets the Bible apart from all other books. In simple societies and in times gone by, people thought that each biblical writer almost heard the words of God in his own mind, or perhaps even with his own ears, and simply wrote them down. Over the centuries, however, we have come to understand the Bible in more subtle ways. We now realize that we are using translations of translations of the original text and we have moved away from the idea that the biblical text was virtually dictated by God; we have come to understand that this holy text is the result of an interaction between God and man, that it is a response to a subtle but powerful divine inspiration.

We know that every bit of it may not be literally true in *every* respect. In fact, the sacred authors of a particular text may not have ever even intended to convey a "literal" truth. Nevertheless, the Scriptures communicate to us the Word of God, the Word that God intended us to receive. Obviously, many of the books that comprise the Bible were not even produced by one single writer. The Old Testament books, especially, were often produced by two or sometimes several authors, and some of the books took a very long period of time to achieve their final form. This is clear from the differing styles of each writer. Even the vocabulary used by various writers will be different, and identifying that vocabulary can help us identify the different writers. There is nothing wrong in saying that many of the Old Testament books gradually grew over the course of time. Does this mean that they were not inspired? By no means! They were simply inspired in a different and subtler way than people originally supposed. Once we become aware of this, the Bible is on its way to becoming an important part of our prayer life.

> The Scriptures communicate to us the Word of God, the Word that God intended us to receive.

The New Testament books are different from those that comprise the Old. Each of them is much more the work of a single writer, or a very limited group of writers, and these books were produced over a much shorter period of time. It is clear in the New Testament that the writings identified as those of St. Paul are his own unique work and style. This also seems to be obvious in the unique and beautiful Gospel according to St. John. The other Gospels, as we have them, may be the work of one or more authors — but we can rest assured that the ancient Church has given us these words, which are guided by the Holy Spirit and are, in fact, the word of God.

This more subtle communication of God's word is sometimes difficult to accept for people who are used to a more basic view of inspiration. Some such people often assume that the New Testament was created whole and entire at a very early date. There are even people who imagine that the apostles themselves used the New Testament writings, when in fact, the New Testament was not completely codified until the 400s A.D. An old gentleman is reputed to have said, "If the King James Version was good enough for Jesus, it's good enough for me." This shows what happens when we approach things too literally and attempt to apply human standards to God.

The truth of God and the knowledge of Christ is given to us by the Scriptures. We then make an act of faith in accepting this knowledge and this truth. Pope Benedict XVI has written that to begin studying the Scriptures is to acknowledge them as the word of God.

Living Daily with Scripture

In many books that I have mentioned, including my own, we find ways to appreciate and to live daily with Scriptures. There are, however, several problems concerning praying with Scripture.

Among the first of these is the temptation to equate the Word of God with the written word. This is ultimately a mistake, one that many Christians make and many Jews before us have also made. We must be careful to remember that, although the Word of God can be expressed through written words, it is never identical with any written words. The Word of God speaks of God Himself, and when we use the Scriptures with reverence and respect — when we use them prayerfully — we can expect the Holy Spirit to work within us to help us understand and to grow in the knowledge of God.

The second problem is that we sometimes confuse a familiarity with the Scriptures, or even a broad but superficial knowledge of them, with a prayerful reading of them. The first is something anyone can achieve, even an atheist; the second involves entering into a prayerful relationship with God. It involves humility and trust — a willingness to turn oneself over to the Holy Spirit, to be led by God into those deep areas where prayer is found and accomplished.

> The words of the Bible must be approached in a special way or they are likely to be misused.

It has been said that the Devil himself can quote the Scriptures; this statement should remind us that the words of the Bible must be approached in a special way or they are likely to be misused. Throughout history, people who called themselves Christians of various kinds — Catholics, Protestants, and Orthodox — have quoted Scripture against one another. Scripture has been used as a weapon to attack and condemn. This is never right, and it is a great misuse of the Bible. The Bible can be an inexhaustible source of prayer and meditation, of learning about God's love for us and His plan for us, but it is never ours to use as we will. It is never our personal possession, but one of God's great gifts to the entire Church. Therefore, we must approach it with the mind of the Church, aware that the Fathers of the Church as well as innumerable saints, scholars, and theologians have preceded us. When we enter the world of the Bible we walk on holy ground and we follow in the footsteps of countless others.

In your life, whether you are Catholic or Protestant or Orthodox, let the Word of God grow in your mind. This is not simply an operation of intelligence. It is something that profoundly involves the heart as well, and it must include a confrontation with our own selves and our sins and shortcomings.

We encounter many potential dangers when we pray with the Scriptures. Like all types of prayer there is the possibility of distraction or boredom. Many parts of the Holy Scriptures become overly familiar to us because we have heard them so many times before, whether we have read them ourselves or heard them at Mass. Usually these are among the most important parts of Holy Scripture, the very parts the Church wants us to focus our greatest attention on. In regards to this Romano Guardini, one of the great spiritual writers of the twentieth century, has said the following. It concerns listening to Scripture read during the liturgy but also can certainly be applied to Scripture read outside the liturgy:

> We must listen with minds alert and hearts and souls receptive. Such listening is all the more necessary because we've heard the words countless times. We are so used to them that they do not easily impress us. We

are convinced that we know all about the Sermon on the Mount, Jesus' parables, or the Epistles, and so when they are read we nod as if to say: "All right, all right — I know." We have to overcome this tendency or our souls will become like a dirt road over which countless feet and wheels have passed, hard-packed and incapable of receiving a single seed.[29]

This is absolutely vital. Every Christian who reads Holy Scripture must read these divinely inspired words afresh each and every time. As I said in the beginning of this chapter, the Bible is a book like no other. Therefore, we must read it in a way that is unlike any other book.

LECTIO DIVINA

God's word found in Holy Scripture can greatly enhance the prayer life of any Christian, but how does the Christian approach Scripture prayerfully? How does someone who may not have formally studied Scripture proceed? Unfortunately, Catholics often tend to shy away from the regular reading of Scripture — perhaps out of a fear that they might not be prepared for such reading, or perhaps because they're afraid they will drastically misinterpret the words of the Bible. Although we should always be careful when we approach Holy Scripture, we should not hesitate in this way. If we read the Bible with the mind of the Church, we will be in no danger of going far wrong and the riches we will gain are incalculable.

There are, of course, many ways to approach the reading of the Bible. You might want to slowly read and mediate on the Scriptural readings for each day's Eucharistic celebration. You might prayerfully and slowly read one of the gospels, bit by bit, over an entire year, lingering on every sentence and paragraph. In a way, the Church does this for us: presenting us with the slow, steady reading of one of the Synoptic Gospels each year, starting on the first Sunday of Advent and ending on the Solemnity of Christ the King. Perhaps we could devote our time to the psalms, every one of which is already a beautiful prayer. Or we might turn to the prophetic literature of the Bible, letting Isaiah, Amos, or Micah become our guides as we try to pray with Scripture. Each and every one of these approaches is potentially beneficial, and they are just some of many ways of praying with Holy Scripture.

Here, however, we will be discussing one specific approach that has been used by the Church since its early days and has recently gained great popularity — a way of praying with the Scriptures that comes out of the Benedictine tradition and is usually referred to by the Latin term *lectio divina*. Probably best translated as "divine reading," this method approaches Scripture in a way that far surpasses the kind of reading most of us are used to. To engage in *lectio divina* is to use the reading of Scripture to open oneself up to the whisperings of God.

St. Benedict, the father of Western monasticism, wrote that we must hear "with the ear of our hearts." This is precisely what *lectio divina,* when done properly, helps us to do.

For those who wish to pray with the Scriptures, a cultivation of interior silence is vital, because it is only in that silence that we are able to hear the voice of God.

We have already spoken often here of the problems posed by the clamor of the world to the person who desires to pray. For those who wish to pray with the Scriptures, a cultivation of interior silence is vital, because it is only in that silence that we are able to hear the voice of God. Our first step, therefore, is to calm ourselves, to become silent and receptive to whatever God has to say to us at that particular moment of our lives. We must turn away from noise, even (perhaps especially) the noise of our own thoughts. We then begin to read a passage of Scripture slowly — in fact, as slowly as possible, dwelling on each word, every phrase. As we read in this way, we do not analyze or interpret. We do not even let our own ideas intrude. We simply remain open, letting God speak to us as our heavenly Father wishes to speak through the particular Scriptural words that we are reading.

We don't need to read much. We may, in fact, read very little: a sentence or two or perhaps a short paragraph. Under certain circumstances, we may find it best to concentrate on only a few words or phrases.

When we come across a word or passage that seems to speak to us in a special way, we stop to ponder it. In doing this we take as our model the Blessed Virgin Mary "pondering . . . in her heart" (Luke 2:19) the birth of Christ. This is the second step of *lectio divina,* and it is rightfully called the stage of meditation. We repeat over and over again the passage of Scripture through which God seems to be speaking clearly to us, letting it touch us on as many levels as possible. It is important to offer no resistance to what we think God is telling us but simply to be open to it. Through meditation on the words of Scripture, we allow God's word to become His word specifically for us, at this specific moment in our lives.

Slowly, we move from reading to meditation, and then from meditation to prayer. This type of prayer is very receptive, which may not be easy for us. We must be aware that this is not a time to barrage God with words. It is instead a time of listening to God, of entering into a gentle dialogue that lets God take the lead. It is also a time to offer Him all our hurts and disappointments, to offer them to Him as we ponder the Scriptural words in our *lectio*. Through these words, we try to let God touch us; we try to let these words transform us.

The final step of *lectio divina* is to enter into real contemplation. This becomes a letting go of words and thoughts; it is accomplished not through our own effort; we let God transcend the words we read and bring us into the Divine Presence.

The point of *lectio divina* is simple. It is merely to be with God in a stillness interrupted by nothing more than the holy words of Scripture. It is to let God remove the barriers between Himself and us, one by one, until we are as open as we possibly can be to the movement of God's Holy Spirit.

Lectio divina involves a progressive surrender — a surrender of our own words, our own desires, and the ideas and concepts we would like to pursue. It is an acceptance of God's will in our lives, in our prayers, in our souls. Modern men and women, so dependent on words, so desperate to make their own voices heard above the clamor of contemporary life, may find such an approach problematic. Yet there are few approaches to praying with the Scriptures that can offer more. I urge all my readers to learn more about *lectio divina* and to make a genuine effort to incorporate it in some way into their prayer lives. I believe the rewards can be enormous.

CHAPTER NINE

LISTENING TO GOD

"Speak, [Lord,] for thy servant hears."

— 1 Samuel 3:10

Throughout religious history, especially the history of Judaism and Christianity, there has been a constant, universal theme of God making Himself known to His children. It can be considered, in fact, the theme of the Bible. Throughout the Scriptures, we read one story after another of God's search for His human creation, of God's efforts to speak to people.

> Throughout the Scriptures, we read one story after another of God's search for His human creation, of God's efforts to speak to people.

An unknown god calls to Abraham, telling him to leave his country, telling him that this god will take him to a land he has never seen and will make of him a great nation. It is Abraham's trust in the words of this god that enables the great story of faith that we call the Old Testament to exist.

Moses hears the voice of God coming from a burning bush, a bush that is ablaze but is not consumed. From such a lowly source, God's own voice issues. Thus begins the liberation of the Israelites from Egyptian bondage, the choosing of Israel to be the bearers of faith in the one true God.

The prophet Elijah, determined to hear the voice of God waits as wind blows, as earthquakes shake the ground beneath his feet, as fire blazes. Finally, the voice he yearns for comes to him in the smallest of whispers.

Mary hears the voice of God coming to her through an angel, an angel who seems to offer her only danger and ostracism, who seems to offer her the impossible. Most people would have rejected this angelic voice; she doesn't, and salvation comes to all humankind.

God communicates with us. This is one of the important messages of the Bible, of our faith. Unfortunately, in the comings and goings of religious activities, this supremely important fact is too often overlooked. It must not be, for it is essential. Without such communication, we could know nothing of God. Without such communication, there could be no prayer.

But of what does this communication consist? How can we perceive it? How do we know when it happens?

To be aware of the communication of God requires thoughtful and extremely sincere movements of the heart. It requires quiet and a willingness to be spoken to rather than to speak. In the words of Blessed Mother Teresa, "God speaks in the silence of the heart. Listening is the beginning of prayer." But listening is usually difficult, and it takes time. The nineteenth-century Danish Protestant religious thinker Søren Kirkegaard has some wise words to offer us as we attempt to listen to the voice of God:

> The "immediate" person thinks and imagines that when he prays, the important thing, the thing he must concentrate upon is that God should hear what he is praying for. Yet in the true, eternal sense it is just the reverse: the true relation in prayer is not when God hears what is prayed for, but when the person praying continues to pray until he is the one who hears, who hears what God wills. The "immediate" person therefore ... makes demands in his prayers; the true man of prayer only attends.[30]

We human beings are mostly "immediate people." We want things right away; we want our will to be done and often mistake our will for God's. We are noisy creatures, and our fast-paced world makes silence and listening very difficult. People involved in other activities of religion, many of them highly virtuous and helpful, may try to allow such activities to take the place of the silent listening to God that is so essential if real prayer is to happen. But this is a great mistake, and every Christian must make every effort to guard against it.

Every day in the Liturgy of the Hours, the Church repeats: "If today you hear His voice, harden not your hearts." In this line from the Ninety-fifth Psalm, and in countless other ways, Christ constantly says to us, "Follow me." In his earthly life, He said this to the apostles and He continues to say it to all humankind today. We must realize that we can only follow Him if we are willing to listen to Him. We must remember that our Lord

Every day in the Liturgy of the Hours, the Church repeats: "If today you hear His voice, harden not your hearts."

seriously criticizes "those who have ears yet do not hear and eyes but do not see" (see Mark 8:18).

I am sure that many of the people reading this book have had their own personal experience of listening to God. These may not be experiences on a very profound level. Don't worry; the fact that they exist at all is what's important. We all understand that the voice of God does not come to us audibly. We have already mentioned some of the ways God speaks to us: the beautiful world around us, our interaction with very good people, teachings we find in the Scriptures and solid spiritual books, the Divine Liturgy of the Church, and especially, reception of the Sacraments. In all of these, if we want to, we can discern the voice of God. Each one of these is an invitation for us to respond fully and joyfully in prayer.

FOLLOWING GOD'S WILL

Early in our spiritual lives, we begin simply, by fulfilling the duties and obligations that God or His representative, the Church, give to us. We must trust the Church to understand far more than we ever could on our own, to be able to interpret the will of God for us well and accurately. Oftentimes we need to follow and be obedient as we try to perceive the will of God. We need to put our own will aside — a very difficult thing for most people to do, not just individually but as a culture. The individual will, the "sovereign self," is exalted in our world. We are supposed to depend almost totally on our selves, on our own ideas, our own experiences. To be a Christian, however, is to acknowledge our dependency on God and to acknowledge that God is in no way a function of our selves — that God is infinitely more than anything we can imagine.

We must always remember that it is surprisingly easy to mistake our own will for the will of God, our own ideas of right and wrong for God's law. Even when we're doing our very best we're likely to make some mistakes. But if we follow the Church's lead and seriously attempt to be docile to the will of God, we have done the most important things, and the rest will come in time. On the other hand, if we are filled with our own self-will, we will surely not be able to listen to God clearly. The voices of the world and of our own desires will drown Him out, for God speaks to us softly. When this happens, we are likely to grow further and further away from God and further from a life of prayer.

Although discerning the voice of God can be difficult, we can take comfort in the fact that as someone's spiritual life progresses, he or she will gradually become increasingly aware of God calling. This is an intuitive awareness and is part of the spiritual lives of many.

BUT WHAT OF GOD'S SILENCE?

As we try to listen to the voice of God, it becomes important not to become discouraged. The life of prayer is subject to many ups and downs, to periods that seem very fertile and to others that seem dry and sterile. We have already discussed this to some extent, but it's such an important topic that we shall return to it again here. Everyone who prays must accept the fact that there may

> Everyone who prays must accept the fact that there may be times when it seems that all we can experience of God is His silence.

be times when it seems that all we can experience of God is His silence.

In the life of the truly prayerful person, however, this is a mysterious kind of silence, one that is often paradoxically full. It is not too much to say that the very silence of God mysteriously draws us to Him, speaks to us in ways that cannot be explained in words. You can love someone and be very close to that person despite the fact that he or she may be far away from you. That person's absence calls out to you. This can sometimes be a more powerful experience than one in which you are actually with the person and constantly talking to him.

There is no doubt that God sometimes seems to be at an enormous distance from us, and the feeling that God is missing from our lives is strong at times in the lives of many people. The coldness of the heart and distraction of the mind that must affect a person who desires to please God and to follow Christ humbly, but who feels constantly alone and abandoned, may be very powerful.

Mother Teresa experienced something akin to what St. John of the Cross, the famous Carmelite saint, described as the "Dark Night of the Soul." This is an advanced mystical experience in which God's purifying love is perceived as darkness. The soul often feels abandoned and cast off. While most of us never experience this phenomenon, we nevertheless may experience similar feelings and must push through those times when we experience the feeling of abandonment and distance from God. Let us take the saints as our guides in this matter and do our best to continue to pray and listen.

STEPS TO LISTENING TO GOD

In my book *Spiritual Passages,* I have tried to explore the various steps involved in trying to listen to the voice of the Lord. Very briefly, I will sum them up for the present reader:

1. We must be convinced that God cares about us, and by His divine grace and Scriptures, tells us so every day of our lives.

2. We must practice silence and recollection to hear the voice of God within us. A distracted person — even a devout person in a distracted experience — is not likely to be aware of God's inspirations.

3. If we experience what seems to be the distance or even the abandonment of God we must follow the example of the saints. We must persevere and never give up. One must even consider the experience of Jesus on the cross, when He cries out, "My God, my God, why have you abandoned me?" If the feeling of abandonment comes, we must strive to remember that we are not alone, that God is still with us even if we cannot sense His presence. We are Christians, and we must carry our cross as Jesus carried His.

4. We must try consistently to fulfill the Divine Will as much as possible in our lives. This is often particularly difficult when we believe that we have undertaken to do God's will and the experience has proven to be unrewarding and difficult for us. We can easily give up under these circumstances. Many examples found in Scripture, beginning with the life of our Lord, tell us to go on even in the face of apparent failure or loss. We must make use of such examples as well as examples found in the lives of the saints to give us the courage to go on.

5. Our prayer must always be joined with prayers of
petition asking the Lord to be with us and to give us
through the Holy Spirit the grace to go on.

The important thing to remember is that our God is
a God who yearns for us, who loves us and is constantly
calling to us. We do not have to depend on our frail and
very fallible ability to listen to God. We must instead do
exactly what Abraham, Moses, Elijah, Mary, and so many
great saints did: place our trust in the voice of the One who
is speaking to us.

> We must never
> feel that we don't
> know how to pray
> properly or that
> our prayers
> are meaningless.

A person who has turned to God in
prayer, even if he is mistaken in various
facts or doesn't have all the information
that other people have, will be heard by
God. We must never feel that we don't
know how to pray properly or that our
prayers are meaningless. We don't have
to pray perfectly because Jesus constantly waits for us at the
well. Jesus understands our prayers — those we utter and
those we cannot give words to — infinitely better than we
ever will. He is speaking to us at every moment of our lives
and listening to all our words and thoughts, understanding
perfectly what we need and want, transforming our feeble
prayers and making them acceptable to Him and to
His Father.

THE EXAMPLE OF HELEN KELLER

You may consider it odd, but when I think of prayer, I often
think of someone who is not usually associated with the
topic: Helen Keller. In fact, I have written about her from

time to time. This woman lived many years without any ability whatsoever to hear or see. She never had either of these experiences that all the rest of the world depends on so completely. Quite accurately, we can say that she did not have even a clear understanding of what sound, light, or color meant. Nonetheless, she was able to communicate well with others — even to speak on the radio. She was able to converse with people on a deeply meaningful level.

Helen Keller was a religious person, and like all the other information she received in her dark world, she had to get her religious information from the people around her. You and I might not agree with the particular forms of Christian belief that she had, but we must remember that she had to depend totally on her teachers, who were doing the very best that they could. The important thing was that this person who lived in darkness was not "in darkness" at all. She was very aware of God, of God's infinite light. Helen Keller, who didn't really understand or follow traditional Christianity fully, was in touch with God. She listened to God often, although she could listen to no one else in her otherwise silent world. We can even say that, in some mysterious way, this blind woman was able to "see" the presence of God around her.

Each one of us, in our own way, must find a way to do what she did: to listen, to follow God's promptings, to continuously form our own unique relationship with God. We have many advantages over Helen Keller. We also have Christ, the saints, and the teaching of the Church. What more do we need to listen to the voice of God? The most important thing for us to do is to open our hearts to God, listen to that "still small voice," and humbly obey.

CHAPTER TEN

PRAYING WITH THE BODY OF CHRIST

"I am the vine, you are the branches. He who abides in me, and I in him, he it is that bears much fruit; for without me you can do nothing. If a man does not abide in me, he is cast forth as a branch and withers."

— John 15:5-6

A TIDAL WAVE OF PRAYER

Obviously, a great many people of many different denominations and even religious faiths will have the experience of God's presence in their lives. Not only do I know this theoretically, but I have experienced it many times in my life in ecumenical and interfaith activities. I also experienced it years ago, traveling and teaching in the Far East and in Muslim and Buddhist countries. Wherever you go, you will find people of many different faiths and backgrounds, of different educational levels and different cultures, turning to God and trying to hear the voice of God.

There is, however, a very special understanding — indeed a unique understanding — of prayer, of listening to and experiencing God, in the Roman Catholic Church because of the sacraments and the teachings of the Church that have grown out of the Scriptures and have been guided by the bishops, primarily the Bishop of Rome.

> We never pray alone because the entire Church, the Mystical Body of Christ, prays with us.

In the early pages of this book, I said that we never pray alone because God always prays with us. This statement was and remains absolutely true, but it's not quite finished. It is now time for me to add to that statement, to complete it: We never pray alone because the entire Church, the Mystical Body of Christ, prays with us. Just meditate on that statement for a moment or two and I guarantee you that you will be overwhelmed. It is almost inconceivable — yet through the grace of God, it's true.

We must keep in mind that each member of the Church, the Mystical Body of Christ, is intimately united with all other members through Christ Himself. As St. Paul says, speaking of Christ, "He is the head of the body, the church" (Colossians 1:18). He also tells us, "We, though many, are one body in Christ" (Romans 12:5).

St. Paul's words are not the only words we have that assure this amazing reality. Jesus Himself said:

> "I am the vine, you are the branches. He who abides in me, and I in him, he it is that bears much fruit; for without me you can do nothing. If a man does not abide in me, he is cast forth as a branch and withers."
>
> — John 15:5-6

These and other biblical statements show the true nature of God's desires for us. They show that God wants the ties that bind the members of the Church one to another to be powerful bonds of love, love that originates in the limitless heart of Christ.

One way the Church can be understood is through the term "Communion of Saints." This is not to say that everyone you see at Sunday Mass is on the fast track to canonization. It is simply a term that defines the Church as being composed of three distinct but intimately related groups: the faithful on earth who hope for heaven, the blessed who have departed earthly life and are in heaven, and the souls in purgatory, who will one day know the joy of heaven. Those among my readers who recall the days before the Second Vatican Council will probably remember another way of referring to that tripartite division of the Church: the Church Militant, the Church Triumphant, and the Church Suffering.

These groups are distinct, yet they are also one. They unite in prayer and intercession. The faithful on earth pray and intercede for each other while also praying for the souls in Purgatory. The saints in heaven are in constant prayer for those on earth, and those on earth pray to the saints for their aid and intercession. Even the souls in Purgatory participate through their prayers for the living, though they cannot pray for themselves.

It is this that makes Catholic prayer so different from all other forms of prayer, for it is prayer that transcends the individual. Each time we pray, our prayers are not a mere trickle, a tiny outpouring from one isolated human soul. Our prayers instead form a huge river, a tidal wave of prayer, one that begins in the heart of Christ and reaches out to all of us, uniting our prayers and praises and petitions with those of countless others, from the greatest of saints to the lowliest of repentant sinners. Christ, in turn, then presents all these things to the Father.

As you read these words, there are people praying for you. Perhaps they pray for you by name; perhaps not. They may live near you, or they may be on the other side of our planet. None of this really matters. The only thing that matters is that they are united to you in prayer through Christ. Disasters — no matter where they happen throughout our world — are met with waves of prayer by uncountable people united to Christ. It is as if our entire world vibrates, trembles, with prayer constantly, the unending prayer of the Body of Christ.

THE SACRAMENTS CONNECT US WITH GOD

The sacraments are among God's greatest gifts to us. In the sacraments we experience a closeness to God that cannot be achieved in any other way.

We don't need to be overly theological as we contemplate the sacraments here. Rather, we should attempt to focus our prayer lives on these seven great mysteries of the Church, which connect us so intimately with Christ, the Heavenly Father, and the Holy Spirit. As we have already discussed, the Eucharistic Celebration — the Mass — lies at the heart of all Catholic prayer.

> The Eucharistic Celebration — the Mass — lies at the heart of all Catholic prayer.

What we call the Mass is probably more accurately called the Divine Liturgy. It would be good for us to remember that for most of the history of mankind, the Mass did not exist. The consecration of bread and wine to be the Body and Blood of Christ was impossible — an absurdity. It is only through God's love for us that the Mass came into being, and it began at a very specific moment during the Last Supper. Jesus, knowing he had reached the end of His earthly life, said to the apostles, "Do this in memory of me." At that moment, He made them the first priests of the Church and prepared them to be able, through His power, to perform the miracle of transubstantiation — the changing of bread and wine into His Body and Blood — in order that we may be filled by His Divine Presence. In the Mass, we also renew the memory of Christ's holy life, especially His death on Calvary and His glorious Resurrection. Any sincere Catholic or Orthodox person should be aware that prayer in all its forms was radically transformed by Christ during the Last Supper, and that this new and infinitely deep type of prayer must be at the very center of our prayer life. Without it, we starve.

THE MASS OVERFLOWS WITH PRAYER

The Eucharistic liturgy, the Mass, overflows with prayer in all its many aspects and kinds. Surprisingly, more and more Protestants are writing and speaking on the Eucharist as well. The Anglican author Evelyn Underhill (who was extraordinarily Catholic in her thought on the Eucharist) has written the following:

> The Liturgy recapitulates all the essentials in this life of sanctification — to repent, to pray, to listen, to learn;

and then to offer upon the altar of God, to intercede, to be transformed to the purposes of God, to be fed and maintained by the very life of God. And though it is the voice of the Church, nonetheless in it is to be recognized the voice of each separate soul, and the care of the Praying Church for each separate soul.[31]

During the Mass, we find ourselves shifting seamlessly from one form of prayer to another. We begin each Eucharistic liturgy as Catholic Christians should begin all things, by invoking the Holy Trinity. Then, ever conscious of our failures, we turn immediately to the Penitential Rite, praying both as individuals and as a community to be forgiven for our many sins, our constant turning from God to the temptations of the world.

At the end of the Penitential Rite, in thankfulness for God's mercy, we turn to a prayer of praise: the beautiful hymn known as *Gloria*. This is sung or at least recited during every Sunday Mass as well as during the Mass on every feast day. In the words of the Romano Guardini:

[The Gloria] begins with the praise of the angels over Bethlehem, continues with expressions lauding God's glory, then shifts to a kind of litany in which the all-holy Persons of the divine Trinity — above all, Christ — are supplicated, and ends with the solemn naming of the threefold God.[32]

After this prayer of praise, we arrive at what today is usually referred to as the opening prayer, but has traditionally been called the *oracio*, or the Collect. This is a brief and very formal prayer of entreaty, different in each Mass, prayed by the celebrant for the entire congregation. These short prayers often sound austere and perhaps not very important but they are, in fact, of very great importance. About them, Guardini writes:

> All Collects, regardless of content, close with a remarkable sentence: "Through our Lord Jesus Christ, who livest and reignest with God in the Father in the unity of the Holy Spirit, God, world without end."

> Here is the direction we are seeking, the proper relation between the goal, the way, and the power which enable us to take it. The goal is the Father; prayer is a seeking of His face. "The Way" is Christ. The power is the Holy Spirit. This one sentence contains the whole law of liturgical prayer. Its method is the same used by the divine Trinity in the work of our salvation. All things come from and return to the Father. In the Logos, He created the world. When man sinned, Christ was sent into the world to rescue it and restore it to the Father.[33]

After the opening prayer, we turn to the Word of God as proclaimed through Holy Scripture. Prepared by our prayers of penitence, praise, and petition, we hear the words of the Bible, encountering them prayerfully and attempting to be open to their life-changing message. Then, after professing our faith through the words of the Nicene Creed, we turn earnestly to direct prayer again: we bring our petitions to our heavenly Father in the Prayer of the Faithful. The Introduction to the Lectionary, Nos. 30-31, says this about the Prayer of the Faithful:

> In the light of God's word and in a sense in response to it, the congregation of the faithful prays in the universal prayer as a rule for the needs of the universal Church

and the local community, for the salvation of the world and those oppressed by any burden, and for special categories of people.

In other words, in this prayer, usually composed of a series of petitions, we go beyond our own troubles and needs or merely the needs of one small congregation. Instead, we try to gather the needs of all people together and place them before the throne of God, to pray as the Body of Christ — including in our prayers all who suffer, no matter who or where they may be.

> In the Prayer of the Faithful, we gather the needs of all people together and place them before the throne of God.

The Prayer of the Faithful brings the Liturgy of the Word to an end.

With our faith deepened by the Word of God and our prayers for the world, we begin the Liturgy of the Eucharist. As soon as the bread and wine that are to become for us the Body and Blood of Christ are prepared, the celebrant invites us to profound prayer, saying "Pray, brethren, that our sacrifice may be acceptable to God, the almighty Father." We answer, "May the Lord accept the sacrifice at your hands for the praise and glory of His name, for our good and the good of all His Church." In his name and ours, the celebrant then prays a short Collect-like prayer called the Prayer over the Gifts. With the congregation's "Amen," we begin the very essence of the Mass and the greatest of all possible prayers: the Eucharistic prayer — the prayer whose purpose is to unite heaven and earth.

The first part of the Eucharistic Prayer, the Preface, contains elements of both a prayer of praise and a hymn of joy. "Lift up your hearts," the celebrant urges us, reminding us that we must now be single-mindedly focused on God; that, as we begin the greatest of all prayers and prepare to encounter Christ in as direct a way as is possible, we must surrender ourselves totally to God. There is no place here for a divided heart or a distracted mind. Concerning this, St. Cyril of Alexandria, one of the Fathers of the Church, wrote:

> The priest cries out: "Lift up your hearts!" For in this most solemn hour it is necessary for us to have our hearts raised up with God, and not fixed below, on the earth and earthly things. It is as if the priest instructs us at this hour to dismiss all physical cares and domestic anxieties, and to have our hearts in heaven with the benevolent God. Then you answer: "We have lifted them up to the Lord," giving assent to it by the acknowledgment that you make. Let no one come here, then, who could say with his mouth, "We have lifted them up to the Lord," while he is preoccupied with physical cares.[34]

As St. Cyril tells us, we should let nothing earthly weigh us down from this point onward. Now is the time that our prayer must soar to the Father and to the Son who, through His sacrifice on Calvary, has reconciled us to the Father. In the Preface, we remind ourselves of how much God has given us — even to His only Son. Each Preface can almost be considered a list of God's gifts to us. We praise Him for these as well as for the countless other gifts He has bestowed and continues to bestow upon us, and we glorify Him as do the angels, singing "Holy, Holy, Holy," words recorded originally by the prophet Isaiah (Isaiah 6:3). In the Preface of the Mass, we remind ourselves of God's infinite love, the endless ways in which He blesses our lives and calls us back to Him despite our many inevitable failures.

Once the Preface is complete, we truly enter the Holy of Holies. The celebrant prays the Eucharistic Prayer, addressed to the Father through the Son, on our behalf. This is the prayer beyond all other prayers, the only prayer that truly accomplishes what all mankind yearns for: it unites us with God and makes Christ's sacrifice on Calvary present to us. It makes Christ Himself — His Body, Blood, Soul, and Divinity — present to us as the Bread of Life and the Cup of Salvation.

> The Eucharistic Prayer unites us with God and makes Christ's sacrifice on Calvary present to us.

The Eucharistic Prayer, sometimes called the Canon of the Mass (or, in the East, the Anaphora), can be a relatively brief prayer or a very long one. There are many examples of Eucharistic Prayers, with many differences among them. However, all Eucharistic Prayers descend from the simple blessings over bread and wine that Christ uttered during the Last Supper. They are, in their origins, blessings over food, transformed by Christ into something infinitely more; through the words of the Eucharistic Prayer, when spoken by the priest, the presence of the One who declared Himself to be "the living bread that has come down from heaven" (John 6:52) is made real under the form of food — bread and wine.

Thus, during the Eucharistic Prayer, all — priest and congregation — should be in profound awe, profound awareness of the presence of God. In the words of Romano Guardini:

> Through the Consecration, [Christ] comes to us, the subject of an incomprehensibly dynamic memorial, and gives us His grace-abounding attention. In Communion, He approaches each of us individually and says: "Behold, I stand at the door and knock." Insofar as the "door" swings open in genuine faith and love, He enters and gives Himself to the believer for his own.[35]

In the Mass, we find the possibility of prayer at its most intense and most complete. All forms and aspects of prayer are united in the Mass. Whenever we pray, we are turning to God, who is constantly calling out to us. In the Mass we encounter God so deeply, so profoundly, that He comes to us humbly as our food, to live within us and transform us. In the words of Evelyn Underhill:

> [The Mass is] . . . from first to last, a hallowing of the Name of God. It calls man, the head of creation, to join with angels and archangels in adoring God. It opens the doors of the natural world to the coming of His consecrating and saving power. In it the creature offers itself under tokens and without reserve for the purposes of His Will, is fed with heavenly food, reconciled and established in the Kingdom of Love, and subdued to the guidance and fostering care of the Unseen. Step by step, conduct, feeling, will, and thought are quieted and transformed to this great purpose. By serial acts of penitence, self-offering, adoration, and communion, the transition is made from the ever-changing world of use and wont to the world that is unsusceptible of change.[36]

When we receive Holy Communion, most of us — and this includes even priests who regularly celebrate the Eucharist — tend to pay much more attention to our

own individual participation in the
sacramental life with Christ than we
do to our participation in the Mystical
Body of Christ. We pray to Christ: we
prepare to receive Him; we repent in His
presence and ask Him to guide us. Only
at rare moments, however, are we likely
to think of our membership in the great
Mystical Body of Christ.

> As we go forth
> from the Mass,
> we should strive
> to remember that
> we remain part of
> the stupendous
> mystery of Christ's
> Body and Blood.

As we go forth from the Mass, we should strive to remember
that we remain part of the stupendous mystery of Christ's
Body and Blood. We who receive the Body and Blood of the
Lord regularly often forget that, through the Mystical Body of
Christ, we are intimately united not only to the Last Supper
but to Christ's sacrifice on Calvary. This is a mystery that
exceeds all mysteries, a mystery that should fill us with awe
and wonder, that should spur us on to constant prayer and
praise of the God who not only searches us out but who gives
Himself to us in this way. It should also lead us to recognize
His presence in others, especially those who receive Him in
Holy Communion as we do, but also in all those made in the
image of God. The Fathers of the Second Vatican Council
have told us: "For by His incarnation the Son of God has
united Himself in some fashion with every man."[37] This is
something we must never forget.

The Second Vatican Council, and the popes since that time,
have made it clear that any good person who has sincerely done
the best he can to find God has a very genuine hope of eternal
life. It must be admitted that the understanding of salvation has
changed since the earlier part of the twentieth century. As far as
I am concerned, this change is very much in keeping with the

Scriptures and the Fathers of the Church — and very much in keeping with the God we know to be pure love.

THE PRAYER OF PETITION

We have spoken already about the prayer of petition, but we will return to it here, for it is an integral part of praying with the Body of Christ. All members of the Body of Christ are obliged to pray for others. In our union with each other through Christ we must be constantly involved in such prayer, constantly involved with each other. This involvement gives meaning to the prayer in which we ask God for the needs of others and for our own needs, as well.

Obviously, the prayer of petition is a very simple form of prayer, one that is a direct response to the felt needs of the individual. At times we may be inclined to look down on this form of prayer, but we must not. Such prayer is an important and integral part of the prayer that Jesus gave us, the Lord's Prayer. In this great prayer, our Lord offers us His own divine example of the way to request things of His Father:

> "Give us this day our daily bread and forgive us our trespasses as we forgive others who trespass against us. And lead us not into temptation but deliver us from evil."

No matter what way you analyze those words, you must admit that they are words of petition, and they are made by the Savior of the world.

At other times, Our Lord tells people to pray in an intercessory way. The most obvious of these are His words,

"Pray therefore the Lord of the harvest to send laborers into his harvest" (Matthew 9:38). Obviously, this is a prayer for the Church and its work for salvation.

At this point, I would like to suggest steps in petitionary prayer which will make it more in keeping with our whole attempt to pray constantly.

First of all, it is important to realize that you are making a prayer of petition; you must acknowledge before God a human need; it may be your need or that of others. It may even be for the entire body of Christ, or even for the whole world. To acknowledge that this is a specific type of intercession is important. Otherwise, intercessory prayer runs the danger of becoming simply an exercise in anxiety or fear. So, as we begin intercessory prayer, we should say to ourselves something like: "I am praying for this intention before God because I believe it is necessary to have His divine assistance."

> As we begin intercessory prayer, we should say to ourselves something like: "I am praying for this intention before God because I believe it is necessary to have His divine assistance."

When we use petitionary prayer, we always need to pray with trust in God. As I said, petitionary prayer can easily become merely the expression of anxiety, something we must guard against. When this kind of prayer is properly done, anxiety is absent (or at least greatly diminished); it is replaced by trust in God. Implied in all proper petitionary prayer is the idea that I am relying on God's assistance in a given situation, one in which I envision a particular solution that I would like to see fulfilled. I must, however, bear in mind that my will is not the will of God, and so I must always be ready to accept and trust the Divine Will, even if it is contrary to what I think is best in a given situation.

I will give you a difficult example from my own life: several years ago, I was struck by a car and came very close to death. To those who witnessed the accident, there seemed to be little hope. The paramedics and the trauma team did their best, but I was without vital signs for almost half an hour, and the attending doctors wanted to give up and take off their gloves. However, a close friend of mine who was with me, Father John Lynch, urged them to go on, as he was praying desperately to God. Dave Burns, another friend, was there, and he spent those difficult moments on his cell phone, calling one friend after another, urging them to pray that I would survive. Obviously, I did — but suppose I had slipped away, or that the deprivation of oxygen to the brain had been so great that my quality of life had been reduced to near zero? One or the other of these two things should have been the outcome, but neither happened. It was the mysterious will of God that I was to live and to recover reasonably well.

The drama continued to unfold, although I was not aware of it. I remained unconscious for three weeks. I often think back, however, to those desperate initial prayers, many from people I knew, some from those I had never met but who knew me from EWTN or some other source. A great group of people were engaged in intercessory prayer for me. This was the Body of Christ in action! My recovery is, if not miraculous, certainly unexpected. What role did the intercessory prayers of so many play? I cannot say for sure. But I know I am here against all odds.

Such stories leave us with questions: Does God need a whole group of people to push Him? What if only one good person had been praying for me? Would the outcome have been different? I don't know, but I do think that the fervent prayers of concerned people are justified by the very words of our Lord Himself. We also see, in many of the psalms and other quotations from Scripture, that God wants and expects us to ask and to intercede fervently for others. In the Old Testament, we find the remarkable example of Moses holding out his arms with the assistance of others as he was praying for the cause of the people of God (Exodus 17:12). We also find in the Book of Numbers the story of Miriam, Moses' sister, who is stricken with leprosy. "Heal her, O God, I beseech thee," (Numbers 12:13) prays Moses, in what is generally counted as the shortest prayer in the Old Testament. Despite its brevity, this heartfelt prayer works. God hears and heals Miriam on the spot. Throughout the Old Testament, Moses is shown to have enormous trust in God. With trust and faith, long-winded prayers are unnecessary. A devout and sincere request is all that is needed.

> With trust and faith, long-winded prayers are unnecessary. A devout and sincere request is all that is needed.

We should conclude from all this that intercessory prayer involves a combination of trust in God, earnest petition, and the belief that God is able to hear and respond to our needs. It also includes the related belief that God loves us and wills our well being.

We must also be aware of the fact that prayer of intercession is never complete on its own; the prayer of thanksgiving must always accompany it. Giving thanks to God should be naturally connected to petitionary prayer for the devout Christian, but this is something we often forget. It is also an extremely important part of the spiritual life and a necessary part of prayer in general. The great Father Solanus Casey, one who prayed constantly for others, said, "Give thanks ahead of time." This is an expression of tremendous trust in God. Looking at the example of Father Solanus, Mother Teresa, Cardinal Cooke, and other remarkable people who obviously had the ability to intercede for other people; we see that each of them had great trust in God, and each of them was very aware of the need to give thanks to God for His goodness. Each of them was also able to face death calmly and with joy, faith, and trust in God.

I visited Cardinal Cooke when he was so ill that he could no longer even get out of bed; this vibrant, hard-working man had endured illness for years and death was near, yet he was completely at peace. As death approached, he spent his time almost completely in prayer, particularly in intercession for the Church and New York. He had a small monstrance in his room in which the Blessed Sacrament was exposed. I recall sensing a profound trust in God in this man whose great faith was that of that of the Irish immigrants.

The same would be true of Mother Teresa. As she was approaching death, she suddenly became filled with joy and enthusiasm. I visited her shortly before she returned to Calcutta from New York for the last time, and I saw that she had become a different person. She was delightful, laughing, joyful, and she remained that way up to the time of her death. Obviously, her prayers of many decades had borne fruit —

not just for the many others she regularly prayed for but for herself as well.

Although I often served Mass as a young friar for Father Solanus, I never had the opportunity to speak to him about his personal life. He was, in fact, a rather quiet man who didn't share his own thoughts very often. Added to this was the fact that he was not permitted to preach. Yet it was very obvious that he was filled with trust in God, and this was the very clear sign of his prayer. People flocked to him, requesting that he pray for them. Many with serious illness, even those in danger of death, would find that through him, they could find their own trust in God.

We can all learn from these three people who are advanced examples of the spiritual life; they show us a very simple approach to intercession and petition. I believe it can be beneficial to make a list of intercessions for each day. Often, this can be done as a preparation for Mass or even during the Mass itself, which is filled with intercessory prayers for the Church and for the world.

If you are attempting to grow in the spiritual life, don't forget the prayer of intercession or the prayer of petition. It is your duty as part of the Mystical Body of Christ. You may recall that when you were much younger, your prayer was almost all intercession, and perhaps it was self-centered. As time goes on, though, that doesn't have to be the case. Intercession is best expressed for the needs of others. We all know very well that the world around us needs the mercy of God, the guidance of Jesus Christ our Lord, and the inspiration of the Holy Spirit. There is no more appropriate practice for the Christian than to pray for this regularly and fervently.

THROUGH THE BODY OF CHRIST, WE MEET THE ANGELS AND THE SAINTS

Throughout this book, we have turned our attention to praying to God, in particular to God in the three distinct Persons of the Holy Trinity. Yet we are all aware of a different kind of prayer as well: prayer to the angels, and especially to the saints, is well known to all Catholics. Such prayer is very important both to the life of the Church and to the life of the individual Catholic. There has been great devotion to Mary, the Mother of God, since the earliest days of the Church. Prayers to her are very ancient, indeed. Catholics and Orthodox often pray to many other saints as well. But why is such prayer possible? Why is it even desirable? We have only to think of the Mystical Body of Christ to understand the answer to these questions.

Prayer to the angels, and especially to the saints, is very important both to the life of the Church and to the life of the individual Catholic.

Large numbers of non-Catholic Christians, mostly Protestants, are mystified by our prayer to the saints. Often, they see no distinction between adoration and devotion, and so they mistake Catholic devotion to the saints for a form of idolatry or even magic. Sadly, some Catholics (and some Orthodox) occasionally approach prayer to the saints in ways that might encourage such misunderstanding. This is something we must take care not to do.

Approached correctly, however, it's simple for even the most theologically unsophisticated among us to understand that when we pray to a saint, our prayer is very different from prayer directed to God. Prayer to a saint or an angel should involve profound reverence, but it does not — and cannot —involve the acknowledgment of sovereignty that is at the heart of prayer to God.

The Latin word to describe prayer to God is *latria*. It means to do as much as one can possibly do — to extend our adoration to its utmost. Of course, we do not extend this to saints or angels; yet in prayer to saints or angels, we become more aware of God's love for us and the ultimate unity of the Body of Christ both in this world and in the next. We become aware that the saints are alive to us and through the grace of God, present to us. Prayer to anyone but God can never include adoration, or *latria*, for no created being is worthy of adoration. If we adore a created being, we have lapsed into idolatry. But despite this possible pitfall, prayer to the saints is important in our progress in the spiritual life. It is an important part of participating in the Body of Christ.

But what does prayer to our Lady and the saints consist of? Perhaps it becomes less confusing if we use the term "praying with the saints" rather than "praying to the saints." Despite the fact that we don't pray to saints the way we pray to God, we still directly address whichever saint we choose to pray with. We also show that saint great honor. We always understand, however, that a saint is a person, just as we are — albeit a person who has passed from this life into the next, one who has been purified of all taint of sin (or was preserved from sin, as in the unique case of Our Lady), and who exists in eternity in the presence of God.

There is absolutely nothing new in any of this; in fact, we acknowledge it every time we pray the Hail Mary. Just stop for a moment to think of the words, which may have become so familiar that we no longer really hear them: "Holy Mary, Mother of God, pray for us sinners now and at the hour of our death." Here, we speak to our Blessed Lady in a way that is very different from the way that we might speak to God. We speak to her as a person whom we love and a member of the Mystical Body of Christ. We do not ask our Lady to grant any request; it's theologically ridiculous to believe that our Lady (or any saint) might, or even could, do anything independently of the divine will. She lives entirely in the presence of God and is in constant adoration before God. Her will is entirely given over to the will of God. So we simply ask her to "pray for us," which means to pray "with" us — to join her prayer to ours before the throne of God.

Sometimes when people hear of Catholic prayer to saints, they wonder why we try to "talk to dead people." The simple answer is: They are not really dead. As Jesus clearly said to the Sadducees when asked about the resurrection of the dead:

> "Have you not read in the book of Moses, in the passage about the book, how God said to him, 'I am the God of Abraham, and the God of Isaac, and the God of Jacob'? He is not God of the dead, but of the living."
>
> — Mark 12:26-27

The saints are not dead; they are more alive than we are!

Fretting about prayer to saints shows a view of God that is very different from ours, one that emphasizes each individual's relationship to Christ and doesn't see that through Christ we are intimately related to all — both those on earth with us and those who have gone before us into eternal life. It is a view that is blind to the Mystical Body of Christ and ultimately a very deficient view of the reality of eternal life.

Prayer to the saints is so common that we often don't realize how mysterious it really is. The saints are obviously not here with us. They have entered a realm of existence with which we can have no direct contact. Yet at certain unusual moments, people may become profoundly aware of the presence of a saint. Even more rarely do people become aware of those beings we call angels.

At certain unusual moments, people may become profoundly aware of the presence of a saint.

As a distinct category of prayer or mystical experience, we can speak of visions or apparitions. We have all heard of the apparitions of the Blessed Virgin to St. Bernadette at Lourdes, to the three children at Fatima, and at other places around the world and at different moments in time. How do we explain the presence with us of a saint, a human person who has been brought by God beyond life and death as we know them, to the joy of eternal life? Throughout the world, many thousands of people are simultaneously speaking to the Blessed Mother. We know she hears them, but how can we explain this, since she is not ubiquitous? Although God is ubiquitous, present in all places and at all times, no human — even a saint in heaven — can be.

The answer to both questions is that we cannot explain these things, except that it is possible through the Mystical Body of Christ. We can, therefore, only react with amazement at the thought that a finite human being who has entered eternal life can also be present to us again in time and space.

The angels, of course, are even more mysterious. We can know little about them, their life, or their thoughts — and, since they are spiritual beings, we can imagine little about them. They are spoken about in Scripture as present at particular moments and in particular places. Christ speaks of the guardian angels of children as being in heaven (Matthew 18:10). Yet angels are also made present to the temporal and spatial world, as they were at Bethlehem at the birth of Christ and during the Agony in the Garden.

All this may seem to present great problems as we try to approach the angels in prayer. Yet devotion to the angels has been consistent throughout Church history. One of the most famous examples of devotion to the angels is the famous prayer to St. Michael that was composed by Pope Leo XIII:

> St. Michael the Archangel, defend us in battle.
> Be our defense against the wickedness
> and snares of the devil.
> May God rebuke him, we humbly pray;
> and do Thou,
> O Prince of the heavenly hosts,
> by the Power of God,
> thrust into hell Satan and all the evil spirits,
> who prowl about the world
> seeking the ruin of souls.
> Amen.

Apart from visions or actual encounters with saints or angels on earth, which are extremely rare, we may at times experience a "presence" or a sense that an angel or saint is with us. Such an experience happened to me in a very small way when I entered the Chapel of the Daughters of Charity at the *rue de Bac* in Paris.

This was the place where the Virgin Mary appeared to the humble nun Sister Catherine Labouré, imparting to her the design of the Miraculous Medal. I managed to come within a few feet of the seat in which St. Catherine indicated that Mary sat when she appeared to her. That place, right near St. Catherine's incorrupt body, is specially marked and cordoned off. The chapel is a good-sized place, and there were many people in it at the time — yet in the midst of this crowd, a distinct impression of the Blessed Virgin's presence came over me. I offered Mass at a side altar that day and was constantly aware that, in some inexplicable way, the Blessed Virgin had been in that room. It may be my imagination or just a trick of my mind; I'll never know for sure, but it felt very clear and very real. I'm sure such feelings aren't as rare as we might think.

> I offered Mass at a side altar that day and was constantly aware that, in some inexplicable way, the Blessed Virgin had been in that room.

The belief that the saints and angels are not remote from us and can in some way also be present to us has produced a powerful devotion to both angels and saints throughout the history of both the Catholic Church and the Eastern churches. Such devotion has animated the prayer life of countless people, giving them examples to follow and friends in the presence of God. All this is made possible only through the Mystical Body of Christ.

Chapter Eleven

Impediments to Prayer and Aids to Prayer

"And you shall love the Lord your God with all your heart, and with all your soul, and with all your might."

— Deuteronomy 6:4

We have said many times already that prayer in our world in not always easy, but the truth is that it never has been. There are many obstacles to prayer. Some come from outside us; many others come from within. If we are to advance in the life of prayer, we must be aware of these. We must see how they obstruct us when we try to pray, and we must learn how to overcome them.

We must also be aware that prayer in isolation amounts to very little. Prayer is a vital part of the spiritual life, but it is only one part. The person who spends his life in prayer but cares nothing for his neighbors has made a horrible mistake. Our prayer lives should give us the desire and the strength to love others, to help others. Jesus often

> The person who spends his life in prayer but cares nothing for his neighbors has made a horrible mistake.

went into the wilderness to pray to the Father, but then he emerged to continue his work with humankind.

In this chapter, we will examine some typical barriers to prayer and some ways of advancing in the spiritual life.

THE TYRANNY OF TIME AND THE NECESSITY OF SABBATH

Many people prepare to pray. In fact, many people prepare rather diligently. Perhaps they have constructed a horarium and an approach to prayer that they believe suits them quite well. Often, such people make numerous trips to Catholic bookstores and purchase the finest prayer books available. They might buy, as well, some of the writings by the great saints and mystics: St. Teresa of Ávila, St. John of the Cross, Julian of Norwich, or St. Francis de Sales. They are very aware that such things can be of great help as they try to deepen their prayer.

Such books do no one any good, however, if they sit on bookshelves waiting to be opened. And this is a big problem, a major obstacle to prayer.

We have discussed the busyness of contemporary life, the frantic pace at which we all live our lives. We are all over-scheduled. It seems that twenty-four hours are no longer enough to accomplish all we need to get done during a given day. Friends and family members need us. It is our obligation to help them whenever possible. As Christians, we take that obligation very seriously, but this takes up more time. Before we fall into bed at night, exhausted, we try to pray, but it is hard to pray and fight sleep simultaneously. When and how do we actually find the time for serious prayer?

The answer is that we do not *find* the time. We must *make* the time. If we hope to pray constantly, then we acknowledge that it is possible to pray through the many events of our lives. But if we hope for truly prayerful lives we must set aside specific times during which we do not permit the clamor of the world to interfere with our prayer. We must demand these times of ourselves. We must insist on time given only to God. Only if we do this will our prayer grow and develop. Such specific times are the foundation upon which our prayer lives can be built.

> Here is some important news: the universe won't implode if you take a few hours off, retreat from the world, and devote yourself to prayer.

Here is some important news: the universe won't implode if you take a few hours off, retreat from the world, and devote yourself to prayer. When we feel so indispensable that we cannot find time for daily prayer, we have clearly developed an inflated opinion of ourselves. Perhaps we have even turned our own supposed importance into an idol. But don't be discouraged, millions of others feel the same way about themselves; it's only human nature. We must abandon a bit of our self-importance and admit that the world will spin along just fine without us for an hour or so as we kneel before the Blessed Sacrament or pray the Rosary. We must learn to refrain from constant doing and learn to rest in the moment with Christ

One of the great gifts of the Jews to the world was the Sabbath, but before they could give it to the world, God had to give it to them. The Sabbath is a day during which one refrains from doing. It is a day to spend in prayer and contemplation, rejoicing in God and in the companionship of loved ones. It also shows trust in God, for the Sabbath is a day when we do not care for ourselves but allow God to care for us. Of the Sabbath, Heschel writes:

> Six days a week we wrestle with the world, wringing profit from the earth; on the Sabbath we especially care for the seed of eternity planted in the soul. The world has our hands, but the soul belongs to Someone Else. Six days a week we seek to dominate the world; on the seventh day we try to dominate the self . . .[38]

The Jewish Sabbath lasts from sundown on Friday night until one hour after sundown on Saturday night. During that time, devout Jews do no work at all. Of course, Christians celebrate their Sabbath on Sunday, the day Jesus rose from the dead. It is an unfortunate fact, however, that in recent years many Christians, including many Catholics, have lost a sense of Sabbath. They often feel that as long as they get to Mass sometime over the weekend, they can treat Sunday exactly like every other day. This is a great spiritual loss. It demonstrates a profound misunderstanding. It shows a sad forgetting of the Third Commandment: "Remember the Sabbath day and keep it holy."

In our prayer lives, we need a multitude of "little Sabbaths," several short Sabbaths every day. They may range from a few minutes of mental prayer to an hour or so spent before the Blessed Sacrament. But they must be inviolate. In the traditional Jewish Sabbath, it is a sin to do even the smallest act of work on the Lord's Day. We don't have to be that severe with ourselves, but we must remember that these little Sabbaths we make for ourselves are moments we offer to God. Can rushing to the drycleaner's or the supermarket really compare with that?

In the Gospel of St. Luke, we read the familiar story of two sisters, Martha and Mary. When Jesus is a guest in their home, Martha is the perfect hostess. She works hard to make sure that the food is good and that Jesus' every material need is satisfied, but in doing so she fails to listen to Jesus as he speaks. Mary, on the other hand, forgets totally about serving food and wine. Instead, she sits at the feet of the Son of God and listens attentively to his every syllable. We see both sisters as being good people, but we know that Martha, for all her good intentions, has made a grave error. She has elevated the things of this world over the Word of God.

We are all guilty of being Marthas. We work constantly to provide things that will not last. We must make the time to pray, to listen to the Word of God. Among the things of this world we must take specific times to give ourselves to "Someone Else." Only in this way will we be given things that do last.

THE WORLD IS TOO MUCH WITH US

We have already discussed the noise of the world, the endless chatter with which our culture bombards us. This is not only an impediment to prayer but an impediment to thought! We must learn to find not only time but *quiet*. We must learn to stop doing meaningless tasks, to slow down, to take a deep breath. Only if we do this will we ever be able to pray.

> We must learn to stop doing meaningless tasks, to slow down, to take a deep breath. Only if we do this will we ever be able to pray.

We must turn off the many devices that our culture loves so much, our cell phones and all the other things that keep us in constant but usually meaningless connection with other people. Texting (it has even become a verb!) has become commonplace. What kind of communication is this? It is a step backwards: tiny messages of a few words zipping back and forth between people. What's wrong with actually speaking to the person you want to communicate with? A text message is a barrier. There is no real contact between people. It is a reversion to the telegram.

Withdrawing from such things is important. It is even more important to withdraw from television. I have known for years that most television programs are silly and useless, and some are even occasions of sin. Who needs it — or, rather, what prayerful person needs it? I rarely watch television; it's a distraction from what is important in life; it's wasting time that could be spent in prayer. Occasionally — two or three times a year, or at the time of some special event, like the pope's election or for some well-announced religious drama or something that is otherwise beneficial — I will turn on the television. But many people don't do this. Many good people, many who have real potential for the spiritual life, waste their time and attention watching mindless drivel or worse. Some things on television can be a kind of spiritual cyanide.

In our times we must develop the ability to discern the good from the bad in the light of Gospel values. We must learn to reject the trivial and turn over and over again to that which is important, not just in our television watching but in all aspects of our lives. We must realize that we are in control; we make the choices of our lives and we must choose the holy rather than the sinful, the important rather than the mundane.

The same as the television — or perhaps worse — is the Internet. I never use it myself. Then how do I know about it? I hear confessions; that's how. Let me tell you: anyone who hears confessions knows more than he wants to know about the Internet. I have learned that many well-intentioned people are corrupted in their minds and souls by this method of communication. Of course, it has many good uses, yet it is a way of bringing inappropriate and often sinful material into your very home or office. Things that once were far from us can now be made present with the click of a mouse. The Internet can be a python that slithers into our homes; it can catch and crush the souls of those who come too close and don't maintain their guard against it. It regularly pulls into its fetid swamp of pornography many good people, especially many young people.

> The Internet can be a python that slithers into our homes; it can catch and crush the souls of those who come too close and don't maintain their guard against it.

Here, we must mention that it is not only those who watch pornography who are in serious danger: those who actually participate and act in it are in a far worse situation. Many young people in today's permissive climate enter into the pornographic world. For some, it is almost a sad joke; for others, it is a desperate attempt at survival. For many, though, it is a seduction, a way to acquire high-quality drugs. It is no coincidence that organized crime runs the pornography industry and the drug industry simultaneously.

One feeds on the other. Each supports the other. One must recognize that supporting pornography in the simplest way, such as watching it on the Internet, is participation in both the spiritual destruction of the souls of others and one's own soul as well.

We live in a world overflowing with distractions, many of them dangerous; a world that makes no distinction between pornography and innocent entertainment; a world that has no sense of the holiness inherent in each human life. In such a world, how do we find the path that leads to holiness? How do we distinguish between the holy and the profane — between the holy and the evil? In our highly sexualized culture, sexual compulsions have become commonplace. They go unrecognized by most people. Yet they destroy lives; they make prayer all but impossible. They distract us from the holy and substitute the depraved. What leads someone out of that to a life that can regain its purity? We have been told, by the highest possible authority, "Blessed are the pure of heart, for they shall see God" (Matthew 5:8).

TWO BLACK CROWS THAT SIT ON THE ROOF OF LIFE

If you are to become a person of prayer, you must regularly ask yourself what you are doing with your life. When you do, you may come up with the answer that most of the time you strive to do God's will, but at times you have occasions of ambition or resentment; this is normal. But if you truly seek a life of constant prayer, ambition and resentment must be overcome. These things eat at the soul. They distract us from prayer; they prevent us from seeing Christ in others. Even very good people among us realize that from time to time they are actually looking forward to hurting someone who has hurt them. They are not planning horrible acts; these are often minor things, but they are very effective at derailing the spiritual things of life. We must personally give up ambition, self-seeking, the need for the recognition of others, as well as the things of the senses that may distract us from our goal.

Ambition and resentment are two black crows sitting on the roof of life, ready to swoop down and change our spiritual intentions. It's very worthwhile to make a regular examination of conscience because of ambition or resentment. St. Paul, in his great statement about love, says, "Love is not jealous or boastful; it is not arrogant or rude. Love does not insist on its own way; it is not irritable or resentful . . . love bears all things, endures all things, hopes all things" (1 Corinthians 13:4-7).

I should probably warn a reader who is trying to root out all the ambition and resentment from his life that this is inevitably a long and difficult struggle. It requires a gradual but complete refocusing of one's own goals in life. We do expect others not to react with resentment or ambition, and when we find such a reaction in another Christian person we are disappointed. Yet, if we look at ourselves, we realize that the same problem is present, as it is to some degree in every human life. Yet these are things that will remove our pure intention and our enjoyment of God's will and prevent us from turning our actions into holy ones, our deeds into prayers.

The person who goes through life not seeking his own accomplishments and not being resentful toward others has the possibility of knowing peace and tranquility, of feeling the presence of God, of entering deeply into prayer. You may occasionally find a lack of resentment and ambition in the life of a very devout person, and you will always find with it a kind of peace that the rest of us yearn for but rarely experience. These people may slip on occasion and fall into minor ambition of one kind or another, but through prayer and repentance, they quickly regain their equilibrium.

> What does it really mean to give up the usual human reactions to hurt and misunderstanding — to just let them go?

Think about it; what does it really mean to give up the usual human reactions to hurt and misunderstanding — to just let them go? That's a great and difficult step, and it indicates the end of real egotism and the beginning of turning one's life into a life of prayer. It is a very normal thing for human beings to desire and appreciate the approval of those they admire and value, and it is a very difficult thing to surrender this as we try to move forward in the spiritual life. The acceptance and enjoyment of the appreciation of others is by no means wrong. However, it can easily get out of hand. We do not walk the road to holiness if our only goal is our personal accomplishments.

These two goals of avoiding ambition and resentment are usually incomprehensible to most people who struggle at the early stages of the spiritual life. It is only later on that a person begins to recognize the importance of this, to recognize how closely this is connected to a life of prayer. There are actually very few people who don't have some kind of reaction to hurt or admiration. We should take comfort in the knowledge that it is an unusual saint who has managed to leave this completely behind. But on those occasions when we enjoy a day without resentment or ambition, we should be able to feel ourselves a little closer to God; we should feel the pure, clean air of God filling the sails of daily life. It will not happen all the time, but we will experience it at times.

Frequently on retreat, we find ourselves in a situation where we resent and are resented by no one; where no one rewards us, nor do we expect to be rewarded. This time of prayer becomes a time of peace and freedom from the attractions of the world. At those moments we perceive life in a different way, a way that is better and closer to God.

It is also wise to help those who are so poor or in need that they are unable to return either their thanks or respect. But even here, there can be a problem. St. Vincent de Paul made the startling and revealing observation that we must love the poor so much that they will forgive us for our kindness to them. That is an amazingly perceptive and revealing comment.

Opportunities for recognition and thanks even come into the lives of many religious people. This begins with the pope and extends all the way down to humblest person in the smallest parish. One must be careful of that. What unites us is the painful reality that we are all sinners and in need of God's redemptive mercy and grace.

It is easy to fall into small sins. One must be careful to do good things that remain totally in secret and will never receive recognition. Such acts are acts of prayer. Once we perform an act for recognition, it can no longer be a totally pure and prayerful act. On the other hand, enduring misunderstanding or accepting the pain of being ignored after having done one's best can be a marvelous opportunity in the spiritual life. It gives us an opportunity to relate to Christ in a very special way.

As we conclude our meditation on ambition, hurt feelings, and resentments, we want to appreciate the fact that each of these can become an opportunity to lift our hearts in prayer. It is prayer in union with Christ Himself. If we read the Gospels carefully, we realize that our Divine Savior was misunderstood almost all the time by His disciples, His contemporaries, and especially His enemies. It is almost unavoidable that He would be misunderstood: as the Son of God, he was not comprehensible by mortal men in the way others were. We must remember that He forgave those who misunderstood Him. Even on the cross, He says, "Father, forgive them, for they know not what they do" (Luke 23:34). We must strive to do the same.

AVOIDING SIN AND DISTRACTIONS OPENS THE WAY TO INNER PEACE

Peace is rare in our world. Inner peace is difficult to attain — so much works against it — yet it is not impossible. In fact, it is what God intends for us. Avoiding sin and distractions must be the first step on the journey to inner peace. Inner peace will grow gradually — painfully slowly, usually only after many struggles and much prayer. It has much to contend with: resentment, jealousy, and sensuality. For some people, even the past rises up to deprive them of peace. The human mind, the gift of memory, works against the quest for peace for some. It reminds them of slights and injuries and even tragedies that remain unresolved in their psyches. These torment and torture them.

> Avoiding sin and distractions must be the first step on the journey to inner peace.

In the mind also reside the mysterious temptations to which we are all prone, the mysterious temptations to turn toward darkness, the temptations that urge us to transform the holy in our lives into the demonic. These must be resisted time and time again. The reward for such resistance is a growing awareness of God, a gradual experience of peace.

There is a wonderful parable that comes to us from the fourth century. In the past, it was often shown in paintings and dramas. Its simple facts leave a powerful impression.

It deals with St. Anthony of Egypt — not the popular friar St. Anthony of Padua, but a hermit. The saint was praying silently in the desert when he was visited horribly by temptations in the middle of the night. It was an assault. Every conceivable sin beckoned to him; his will seemed frail, unable to resist. But he fought back as best he could and just barely prevailed. As the first light of dawn broke over the desert, an exhausted Anthony called out in anguish: "Lord, why have you left me alone? Where have you gone?" The legend tells us that the saint heard these words in response: "Anthony, I have been with you all this time."

This powerful message is one we should tuck away in our minds, for we, like Anthony, will be seriously tempted and will feel alone and unable to resist. These words remind us that we are not alone in our resistance; that God — even when He seems to us to be absent — is with us, always supporting us in ways we cannot imagine.

Rejoicing in the Lord

Since the days of the Charismatic movement there has been an awareness of "rejoicing in the Lord." This actually made a number of people uncomfortable, as they weren't particularly used to being happy in the Lord. These days, the Charismatic Renewal movement has quieted down a bit, although it is still present and has made its contribution to the spiritual life of Christians.

This movement pointed out, however, that religion or faith without joy is deficient. It showed that it is necessary to take some time out to rejoice. But in spreading this advice, we also must remember that some people who don't manifest joy are actually suffering because of physical illness or psychological difficulties, particularly depression. If you tell somebody who is depressed to cheer up and smile, you may inadvertently make him feel worse, not better. Such advice is really meaningless; a depressed person has little control over his depression.

> I am by no means a born optimist. I grew up in Jersey City, a place that never specialized in turning out optimists.

On the other hand, pausing to take into account the many simple and beautiful blessings that God has bestowed upon us is very important. I know it's not always easy to do this. I am by no means a born optimist. I grew up in Jersey City, a place that never specialized in turning out optimists. The idea was to be a realist. We used to say, "The difference between optimists and pessimists is information — the pessimists have it. The optimists don't."

However, to go through life constantly looking at things in a sorrowful or even penitential way is not particularly healthy or in keeping with the Scriptures. The psalms regularly tell us to rejoice in the Lord; on the other hand, the New Testament is certainly not filled with mirth. However, it can be very beautiful and very positive, particularly many of the writings of St. Paul and of St. John.

Standing back from the whole experience, we see that the life of the Christian, as described in the Scriptures, should involve a peaceful, even grateful, rejoicing for the promise of eternal life. If you read the lives of the saints, you will see that in quiet ways they are filled with peace, and that most of the time the saints show a kind of joy in addition to their peace. An old saying attributed to St. Francis de Sales says, "A sad saint is a sorry saint."

As we make our way though life, there will obviously be many dark days. There will even be catastrophes. A person must endure these by joining with Christ on the cross. You will notice when you meet people who have been through terrible catastrophes that human personalities are able to readjust themselves. Very rarely does a person completely fall apart because of disaster or tragedy. I have known people who survived the terrible days of the Holocaust, people who survived severe earthquakes, and even people who have endured terrible acts of violence perpetrated in their own homes by members of their families. Somehow, these people find the courage to keep going. Backed up with the grace of the Holy Spirit, they somehow manage to go on. [39]

RELIGION CAN DISTRACT US FROM PRAYER

Here it comes: the one you didn't expect. For those who have achieved a measure of advancement in the life of prayer, one of the great obstacles to further advancement can be religion itself. Religion, if we aren't careful, can become a series of props for us. We feel we cannot pray properly unless we are kneeling before a specific icon. We pray for the intercession of a special saint and feel we can't exist without it. We love the warm feelings that come from the sound of Gregorian Chant or those marvelous old hymns. When we participate in stately liturgy, we feel close to God.

> For those who have achieved a measure of advancement in the life of prayer, one of the great obstacles to further advancement can be religion itself.

None of these things is wrong in itself. Indeed, most of them are very good. The problem arises when these things become ends in themselves rather than means, rather than aids. They can become little idols. These things make us feel good. They make us feel holy. They make us feel a part of something. They give us the warm feelings that are so popular in our culture. But they can become barriers to advancing in the life of prayer, for prayer is not always consolation, warmth, or a feeling of belonging. Often, prayer can be challenging; it can be dry and utterly without consolation; it may throw us into great turmoil. Christ offers us the cross and eternal life, not sentimentality.

We must remain open to all of this — to following the road that Christ has prepared for us, even when it seems difficult and lonely, rather than wallowing in the sentimental aspects of religion. We must take care that it is Christ we really seek and not simply the comfort of religion. We cannot be like the person who devoutly prays his Rosary as he walks down the street and becomes so lost in this beautiful prayer that he doesn't even notice himself stepping over an old woman who has fallen and needs his help.

We must let ourselves be distracted from these things and from all things by God. This is a paradox. A distraction from one thing is attention to another. We grow in the spiritual life by turning away from all distractions. As we think about God, we are distracted from the irrelevant (or at least the mundane). We must let ourselves be distracted even from the symbols of God, to God Himself.

A LIFE OF PRAYER IS A LIFE OF VIRTUE

For a person to grow in the life of prayer, it is essential that he simultaneously grow in the life of virtue. He has to avoid directly intending to commit any sins — even a small one, such as a white lie. We all are aware of our sins of confusion, weakness, and distraction. They are the things that we ordinarily need to repent of, and the prayer of repentance is for all of us a necessary and very good prayer. Also, even when a person has moved away from deliberate sin and sinful attitudes, little things — small but powerful sins — remain, standing in the way of a life of prayer.

In *The Imitation of Christ,* we are told that if our hearts are pure, then all things will be mirrors of God and of a holy life. The growth in the awareness of God is a growth in holiness. Any other way of attempting to be aware of God's presence is either a psychological trick or an illusion. The teachings of Christ in the Gospel and the other words of the New Testament make very clear that the road to God is through holiness and avoidance of evil.

WHERE THERE IS NO RELATIONSHIP,
THERE IS NO PRAYER

Trying to grow in the knowledge of God and the awareness of His presence is a lifelong project. Perhaps it is more accurate to say that it is the basic purpose of our lives on earth. We are made to meet God. It is our purpose on earth to grow closer to Him — day by day or year by year, our lives should become more open to God's presence; as this happens, we begin to feel that we are "meeting" God.

Every relationship with another person involves encountering that person, whether that means to hear, see, or write to that person. The word relationship is related to the word "reality." When you are talking to a long-distance telephone operator, you may be getting useful information, but you are not in any relationship with her. If on Christmas Day, you say to the operator, "I hope you have a happy Christmas," you may get a human response and so enter slightly into real relationship with her. I sometimes will say to an operator, "God bless you," and on occasion, I even get back a startled "God bless you, too." I'm sure all this must be against the rules of the telephone company, but nonetheless, it involves the glimmer of human relationship. It has made the interaction human for a brief moment.

Apart from such a tiny relationship, there are slightly longer ones that we all experience: a discussion with the nurse in your doctor's office, for example. Oddly enough, physicians often develop ways of dealing with patients that exclude real relationships. This is probably an effort not to waste time and to maintain objectivity and efficiency. They are likely to see a relationship as making things complicated for them.

In our journey through life, we meet all kinds of people. We have relationships with many; most are superficial, but — if we are fortunate — a few will be deep. Anyone who has moved out of the "old neighborhood" remembers they enjoyed real relationships with their old neighbors. Most people hope and expect to keep in touch with such people. Usually, this doesn't happen. The relationships may have been real and even deep, but they are understood on some level to be temporary ones.

Finally, there are relationships in our families and professional situations, where we may have maintained a relationship for an entire lifetime. If we look at such relationships we will discover there are many qualities to them: friendliness, criticism, jealousy, kindness, affection. All such relationships are multifaceted and multidimensional, at times mixing good and bad.

How do we have a relationship with God, with Christ, or with the Holy Spirit?

But now comes the big question. How do we have a relationship with God, with Christ, or with the Holy Spirit? The first problem here, of course, is that we encounter God in ways different from the ways in which we encounter people. As we have already discussed, we cannot see God or touch God. We may feel God's presence powerfully, but there is no physical component in this presence as there is with another person. We can picture Christ, but we have never been in His presence as He walked the roads of Galilee. We have almost no idea of what meeting Him in eternal life will be like. I sometimes ask myself, "What will I say at the Last Judgment when I meet with Christ?" After years of considering this, I've come to the conclusion that I'm not going to say one word. I'm going to let Him do all the talking.

Well, then, what kind of relationship can we have? This is an important question, for prayer is relationship: we don't pray to nothingness; we pray to Someone. If we can't be in some kind of relationship to God, then our prayer will be dead.

We must begin with the belief that Christ is there, that we are truly in relationship with Him. Then, we must be aware that in all that we have said so far, we have implied another aspect to this relationship — our own part. We must not stop at acknowledging Christ's presence; we must strive to follow Him; we must do His will. Jesus said, "Take up your cross and follow me." These are words we must take seriously if we are to be in a relationship with Christ, if we are to be truly prayerful. As we follow Christ, we make a donation of our very selves. When we have achieved the willingness to bend our will — not just occasionally, but on a daily basis — to the will of Christ, we will have entered into the second stage of relationship with Him. We are to give up what is bad, and we understand that it is necessary to do good things, even those things that are difficult and unpleasant to us. If we do this, we build our relationship with Christ.

> We must also become aware that Christ is not only there but in a very specific way is there for us, that He is not only aware of us as individuals but is concerned about us at every moment of our existence.

We must also become aware that Christ is not only there but in a very specific way is there for us, that He is not only aware of us as individuals but is concerned about us at every moment of our existence. I will be the first to admit that this is not easily accomplished. Of course, there are days when Christ's concern for us seems real and present. I remember the days of my ordination and first Mass. Although there were many distractions, I remember being profoundly aware that Christ was there for me that day.

At other very important and difficult moments, I also knew that He was there. When I woke up in the hospital after being unconscious for three weeks, the priest with me explained what had happened: I had been struck by a car and nearly killed. I was unable to speak. I immediately turned my mind to Christ and had a profound sense of His presence. Step by step, it was explained to me that I had actually come to the very edge of death; that I had been without vital signs for so long that the doctors believed that if I ever managed to recover physically, I would be virtually without mental function.

But as all this was going on, something else was going on, too. I was becoming more and more filled with Christ, filled with the understanding that it was Christ who had kept me in this life. I was determined to follow Him as completely as I could in whatever role I was to have for the rest of my life, even if it should be that of an invalid.

We meet people in life who have experienced serious setbacks or incapacities. My receptionist for thirty-five years is a woman who was born with cerebral palsy. She has never been able to walk but has had a very active and engaged life. Those people — like myself — who have been incapacitated later in life can use such people as models in their turning to Christ. Karen, my receptionist, is unfailingly devout. She does not question her limitations but sees in them God's mysterious workings. Seeing her day after day, how could I do any less? She helps me to turn quickly to Christ and to be open to Him.

If you are looking around for a good argument for having faith and religious practice in your life, you don't have to look too far. When disaster strikes, it is the people of faith who go on.

About sixty years ago, Germany was in complete collapse. There was nothing left. Its cities had been turned to rubble; its economy was destroyed; millions of its citizens had been killed. Large numbers of German soldiers were missing in action and no one had any idea how to find out if they were alive or dead. At this bleak time, a young teenager found himself forced (as were all young German men at the time) into the Hitler Youth Corps. He and his brother firmly refused to join the Nazi party and as a result they were physically abused in the barracks. Within a few weeks, the Allies had taken over and the young men were "sent home to their mothers." This boy came from a family that was staunchly anti-Nazi and had suffered much during the Hitler years. The father had lost his job as a country constable, and the family had subsisted on almost nothing. Despite all this, when the war was over, the two brothers immediately went to the seminary and were both ordained to the priesthood in 1951, only six years after the fall of the Nazi Reich.

What an unpromising beginning. Yet, as I am sure you have guessed by now, one of those young men, Joseph Ratzinger, is now the first German pope in history. What had happened to him and his family, and many other loyal German Catholics who did not surrender to the hopelessness that was so prevalent at the time? I once heard a Passionist Father, who had been sent as a missionary to Germany right after the war, claim that the faith at that time was dead in Catholic Bavaria. The lives of the Ratzinger boys prove that this statement was not quite true. It proves that God is constantly calling each of us, and that a life of prayer and faith enables us to discern that call and respond to it. It proves, as well, that no disaster is too great for God to overcome.

CONCLUSION

A CONVERSATION WITHOUT WORDS

And then he told them a parable, to the effect that
they ought always to pray and not lose heart.

— Luke 18:1

Our goal, which is stated in the very title of our book, is to follow St. Paul's famous directive. We have been searching diligently for a way to "pray constantly."

So far, we have discussed many forms of prayer, many approaches to prayer. Ways such as faithfully cultivating our relationship to the Lord, disposing ourselves with attitudes of devotion and surrender, and developing a routine of daily prayer, can help us reach the goal of praying constantly.

And as we grow in the practice of prayer, our communication with God will change from our speaking to him and our listening and responding to his gentle voice. Our prayer will become a conversation with God that has no words — that needs no words. St. John Vianney once asked a parishioner what he said to God during his frequent periods of adoration before the Blessed Sacrament. The parishioner's response? That he didn't say much in words: "I just look at Him, and He looks at me."

If we are to pray constantly, we must distinguish between prayer and prayers, between the conversation that involves words and concepts and the conversation that has transcended such things and has become pure relationship.

Think of the person to whom you feel closest. When you are with that person do you need to fill every moment with speech, with questions and answers, with stories and statements? No. When we spend time with a person to whom we are very close, we often speak very little. Communication comes in other ways — ways that may be deeper than words — in a look or a smile, in the way you might hold your body, in a gesture. Sometimes communication seems to come independently of all these things. Sometimes that person simply knows what is in our mind. Communication just happens.

And so it is with our friendship with God. As we grow closer to God; as we become adept at staying aware of His presence; as we continue to turn away from our sinful behaviors; as we worship faithfully at Mass and join in prayer with all the members of the Body of Christ; and as we bless each day with a routine of prayer, we will experience what it means to pray constantly. We will hunger and thirst for God. And He will take up His residence in us, delighting us by transforming our hearts into His tabernacles.

ENDNOTES

1. Abraham Joshua Heschel, *Quest for God* (New York: Crossroad, 1954) p. 58.
2. *Catechism of the Catholic Church* # 2560.
3. Heschel, p. 58.
4. Richard Rubenstein, *After Auschwitz* (Baltimore: Johns Hopkins University Press, 1966) p. 27.
5. John Shelby Spong, *Here I Stand* (New York: HarperCollins, 2000), pp. 468-469.
6. Emily Dickinson, "Of Course I Prayed," *The Complete Poems of Emily Dickinson*. Thomas H. Johnson, ed. (Boston: Little Brown and Company, 1952), p. 179.
7. Archbishop Anthony Bloom, *Beginning to Pray* (New York: Paulist Press, 1970), p.1.
8. Pope John Paul II, *The Spirit, Giver of Life and Love* (Boston: Pauline Books and Media, 1996), p. 39.
9. Maurice Friedman, *Martin Buber's Life and Work* (Detroit: Wayne State University Press, 1988), p. 99.
10. C. S. Lewis, *Miracles* (New York: HarperCollins, 2001), p. 131.
11. See Paul Tillich, *Systematic Theology, Volume 1* (Chicago: The University of Chicago Press, 1951). The discussion regarding God as "being" is contained primarily in pp. 168-238.
12. The meaning of "human," by the way, is a startling one; it's based on the word "humus," which means soil or dirt. This might not be an image we particularly like, but it reminds us clearly that we are made of the dust of the earth and to that dust we will return in death. It is interesting that in Hebrew, the name of the first person ever created, "Adam," also comes from a root word that means ground or earth or soil. This connection of

human nature to the earth reminds us once again that the divine nature transcends our nature, just as God Himself transcends the material world (the "soil" of which we are made).

13. Jules Harlow, ed. *Siddur Sim Shalom* (New York: The United Synagogue of Conservative Judaism, 1985), p. 275.

14. Fr. Neil Xavier O'Donoghue, trans. *St. Patrick, His Confession and Other Works* (Totowa, NJ: Catholic Book Publishing Co. 2009), pp. 15-16.

15. Joseph Mary Plunkett, "I See His Blood upon the Rose." *1000 Years of Irish Poetry*, Kathleen Hoagland, ed. (New York: Welcome Rain Publishers, 2000), p. 693.

16. Quoted in *Spe Salve*.

17. See Benedict J. Groeschel, C.F.R., and Bert Ghezzi, *Everyday Encounters with God* (Ijamsville, MD: The Word Among Us Press, 2009).

18. *Lumen Gentium*.

19. I would warn you, though, that books written during the '70s and '80s may include attitudes derived from secularism or non-sacramental religious practices. These ideas are far too often applied inappropriately to the Mass, and this only causes confusion. I am happy to say that this kind of thinking is rapidly disappearing, but if you find an old book written during that period, look carefully at its contents before you give it your full attention; make sure it teaches the truth.

20. John Hardon, S.J., *Theology of Prayer* (New York: Daughters of St. Paul, 1979), p. 158.

21. Benedict J. Groeschel, C.F.R., and James Monti, *In the Presence of Our Lord* (Huntington, IN: Our Sunday Visitor, 1996), p.126.

22. *A Catholic Book of Hours and Other Devotions* (Loyola Press, 2007) is a very good shorter version of the Hours.

23. Pope John Paul II, Apostolic Letter *Rosarium Virginis Mariae*, 2002.

24. S.C. Hughson, O.H.C., "The Use of the Rosary" (West Park,

NY: Holy Cross Press, 1918).

25. Timothy Ware, *The Orthodox Church* (New York: Penguin Books, 1964), p. 313.

26. Ibid.

27. Bishop Ignatius Brianchaninov, *On the Prayer of Jesus* (Liberty, TN.: St. John of Kronstadt Press, 1995).

28. Ware, p. 312.

29. Romano Guardini, *Preparing Yourself for Mass* (Manchester, NH: Sophia Institute Press, 1993), p. 76.

30. As cited in George Appleton, gen. ed., *The Oxford Book of Prayer* (New York: Oxford University Press, 1985), no. 790.

31. As cited in Father Benedict J. Groeschel, *The Journey Toward God* (Ann Arbor, MI: Servant Publications, 2000), p. 223.

32. Guardini, p. 83.

33. Guardini, p. 92.

34. *Catechetical Lectures* 848d, St. Cyril of Alexandria, A.D. 350.

35. Guardini, p. 176-7.

36. Underhill, as cited in Groeschel, p. 224.

37. *Gaudium et Spes*.

38. Abraham Joshua Heschel, *The Sabbath* (New York: Ferrar, Strauss & Giroux, 1951), p. 13.

39. For an exploration of this, see my book *The Tears of God* (Ignatius Press, 2009).

NOTES

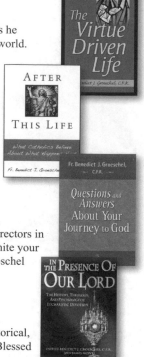